To AJW, of course.
GAP

To my parents.
JDO

Designed and produced by Jacaranda Designs, Ltd.
Post Office Box 76691   Nairobi, Kenya
Copyright (c) by Jacaranda Designs, Ltd.

First published 1992.
Repint 1994

ISBN 9966-884-24-6

Illustrations by James Okello. Text by Gail A. Porter
Typeset in Avant Garde, Palatino and CgDomCasualBd.
Produced in Kenya. Printed in Singapore.

Notes to parents and teachers...

This book is designed to stimulate your child's **love of learning** and **books**, natural **curiosity** and **imagination**.

How to use this book

- Sit comfortably with your child.

- Read aloud to your child enjoying the **repetitive sounds** and the **humour**.

- Talk about the pictures.

- If your child has already started to read, point to the letters with the same sound as you read but without comment.

- Always make your reading together sessions fun. Choose a moment when your child is receptive and in a good mood. Stop if your child loses attention. Never let reading together become a forced lesson or a test!

- Let your child absorb the information naturally.

- Together, look at the full map and find the countries and places mentioned.

- Read the book as often as your child requests (or as often as possible!).

Hugo Hippo's
ABC Fun Book
in Africa

illustrated by James Okello
text by Gail A. Porter

Here's Hugo .....

arriving on an ant in Africa.

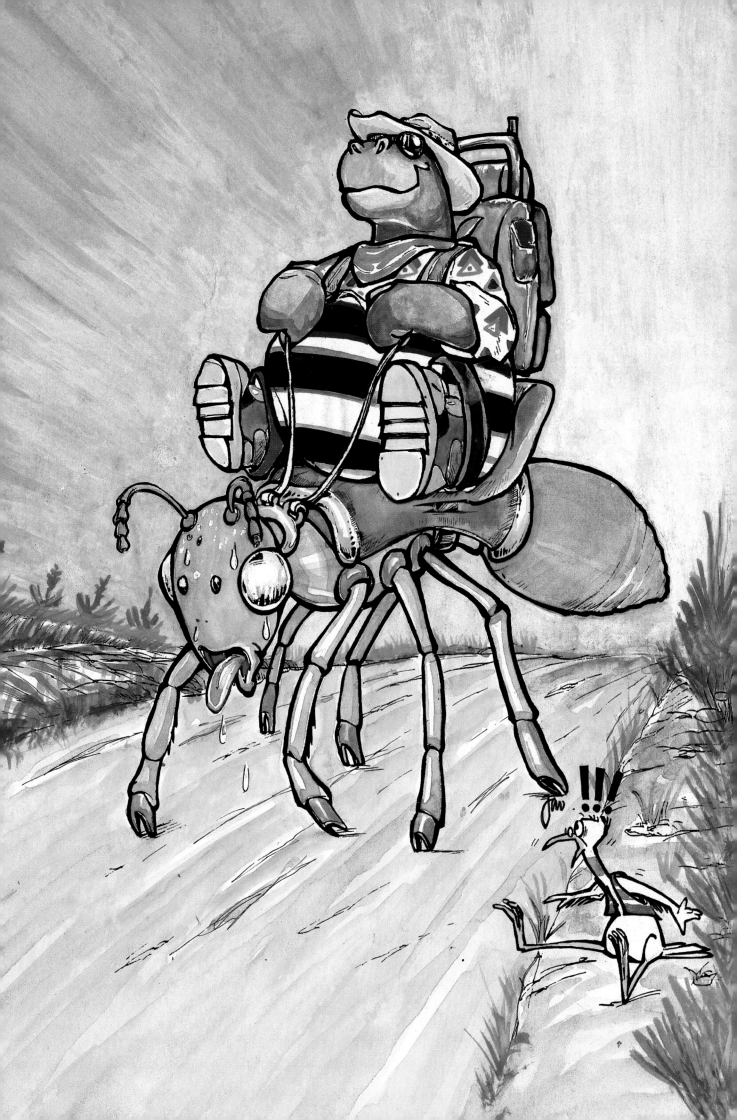

B b

Here's Hugo .....

basking on the beach in Bioko.

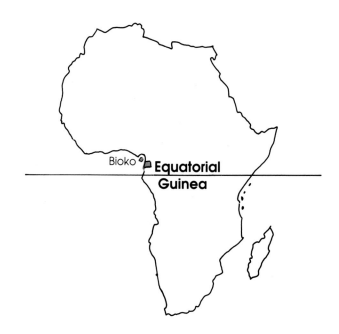

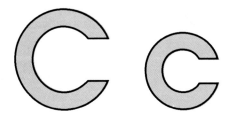

C c

Here's Hugo .....

on a donkey catching a camel in Casablanca.

Casablanca

Morocco

D d

Here's Hugo .....

**driving a dik-dik
to a dance
in Dar-es-Salaam.**

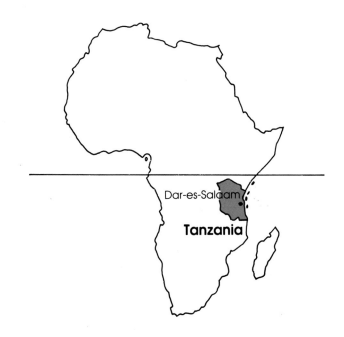

Ee

Here's Hugo .....

**eating an egg
on an elephant
in Ethiopia.**

Ethiopia

Ff

Here's Hugo .....

**frying flies
for his breakfast
on safari in Francistown.**

The Okavango
Botswana Francistown

G g

Here's Hugo .....

**galloping
on a guinea-fowl
in a game park
in Gabon.**

Gabon

Hh

Here's Hugo .....

**hugging a hyena
in a helicopter
over Harare.**

Zimbabwe
Harare

Ii

Here's Hugo .....

**inviting an impala
for a trip
on the Indian Ocean.**

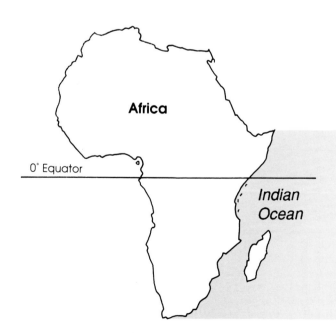

Africa

0° Equator

*Indian
Ocean*

J j

Here's Hugo .....

joking with a jackal in the jungle.

Jungle areas

Kk

Here's Hugo .....

**flying kites
with a kudu in Kenya.**

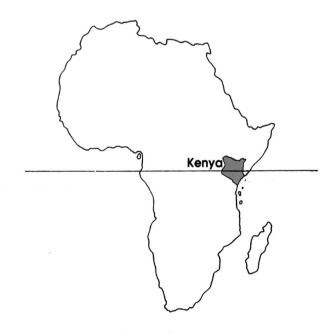

L l

Here's Hugo .....

**licking lollies
in a lorry
on the way to Lamu.**

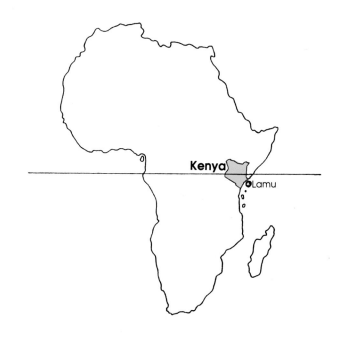

Mm

Here's Hugo .....

**making a mess
in the mud
with a monkey
from Mozambique.**

Mozambique

Nn

Here's Hugo .....

**knitting knee-socks
for his nephew
in Namibia.**

Here's Hugo .....

offering an orange to an ostrich in the Okavango.

The Okavango

Botswana

Here's Hugo .....

**pinging peas
on a thumb piano
in Pemba.**

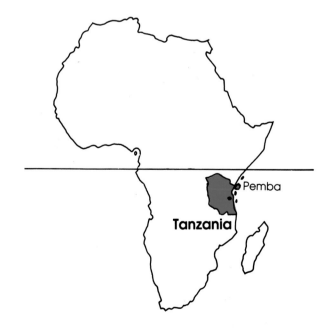

Qq

Here's Hugo .....

**quacking and
squawking
like a duck
on the Equator.**

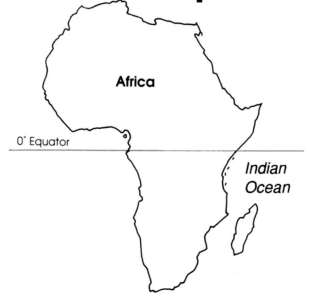

Africa

0˚ Equator

*Indian
Ocean*

R r

Here's Hugo .....

**reading riddles
to a rhino
in Rwanda.**

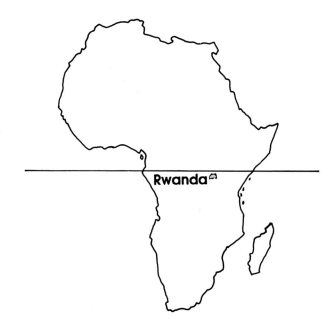

Ss

Here's Hugo .....

stewing seaweed
for his supper
in Senegal.

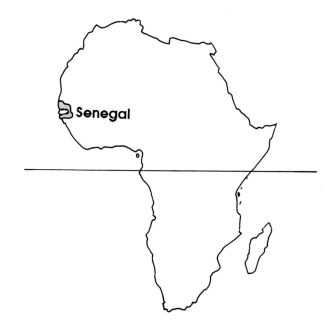

Tt

Here's Hugo .....

**teaching a turtle
a traditional tune
in Tanzania.**

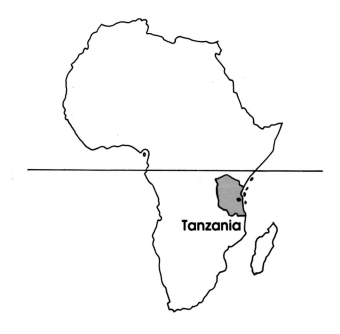

Tanzania

U u

Here's Hugo .....

**uncovering
an ugly buffalo
up-country
in Uganda.**

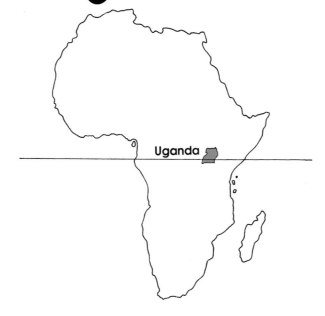

Uganda

Vv

Here's Hugo .....

**driving vultures
over the savannah
near Lake Volta.**

Ww

Here's Hugo .....

**waving farewell
to a warthog
in Western Sahara.**

Western Sahara

Xx

Here's Hugo .....

boxing with a fox in Xai-Xai.

Mozambique

Yy

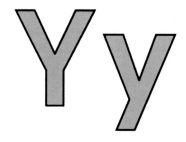

Here's Hugo .....

yelling "Yahoo!" from his yacht in Yawri Bay.

Yawri Bay — Sierra Leone

Z z

Here's Hugo .....

grazing zebras on the shores of Zanzibar.

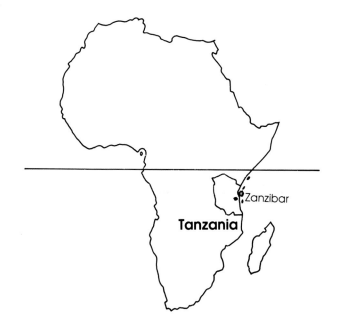

World Map

Our world map shows the big areas of land and water.

The land areas are called 'continents'.

The big bodies of water are called 'oceans'.

Can you find the continent of Africa?

North America

Pacific Ocean

Atlantic

Equator

South Ameri

A

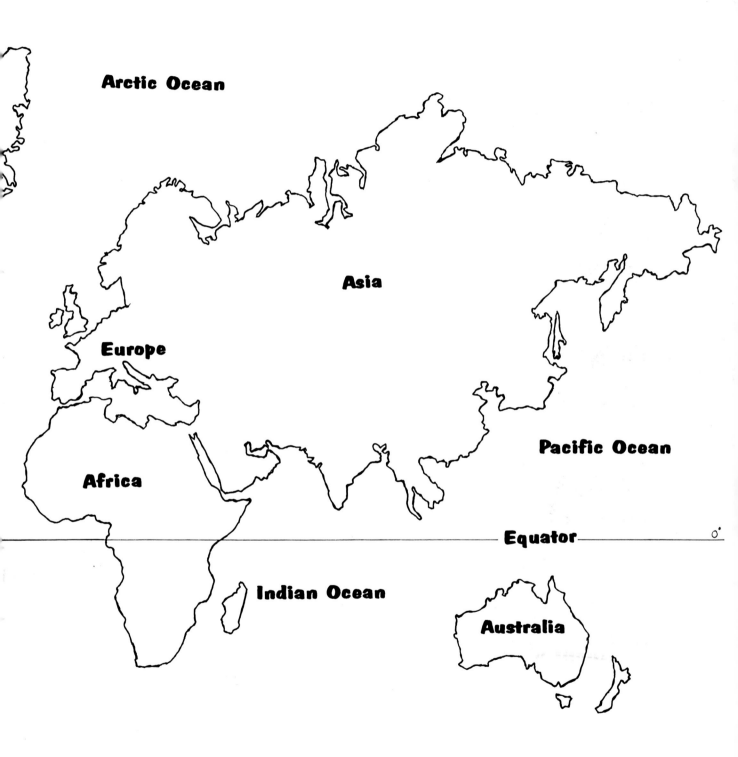

Arctic Ocean

Asia

Europe

Africa

Pacific Ocean

Equator ———————————— 0°

Indian Ocean

Australia

ca

interchange
FIFTH EDITION

2 B

Student's Book

Jack C. Richards
with Jonathan Hull and Susan Proctor

WITH ONLINE
SELF-STUDY

CAMBRIDGE
UNIVERSITY PRESS

CAMBRIDGE
UNIVERSITY PRESS

University Printing House, Cambridge CB2 8BS, United Kingdom

One Liberty Plaza, 20th Floor, New York, NY 10006, USA

477 Williamstown Road, Port Melbourne, VIC 3207, Australia

4843/24, 2nd Floor, Ansari Road, Daryaganj, Delhi – 110002, India

79 Anson Road, #06–04/06, Singapore 079906

Cambridge University Press is part of the University of Cambridge.

It furthers the University's mission by disseminating knowledge in the pursuit of education, learning and research at the highest international levels of excellence.

www.cambridge.org
Information on this title: www.cambridge.org/9781316624029

First published 2006
Second edition 2013
20 19 18 17 16 15 14 13 12 11 10 9 8 7 6 5 4 3 2 1

Printed in Malaysia by Vivar Printing

A catalogue record for this publication is available from the British Library

ISBN	9781316620236	Student's Book 2 with Online Self-Study
ISBN	9781316620250	Student's Book 2A with Online Self-Study
ISBN	9781316620328	Student's Book 2B with Online Self-Study
ISBN	9781316620342	Student's Book 2 with Online Self-Study and Online Workbook
ISBN	9781316620366	Student's Book 2A with Online Self-Study and Online Workbook
ISBN	9781316620373	Student's Book 2B with Online Self-Study and Online Workbook
ISBN	9781316622698	Workbook 2
ISBN	9781316622704	Workbook 2A
ISBN	9781316622711	Workbook 2B
ISBN	9781316622728	Teacher's Edition 2 with Complete Assessment Program
ISBN	9781316622285	Class Audio 2 CDs
ISBN	9781316623992	Full Contact 2 with Online Self-Study
ISBN	9781316624005	Full Contact 2A with Online Self-Study
ISBN	9781316624029	Full Contact 2B with Online Self-Study
ISBN	9781316622254	Presentation Plus 2

Additional resources for this publication at www.cambridge.org/interchange

Informed by teachers

Teachers from all over the world helped develop *Interchange Fifth Edition*. They looked at everything – from the color of the designs to the topics in the conversations – in order to make sure that this course will work in the classroom. We heard from 1,500 teachers in:

- Surveys
- Focus Groups
- In-Depth Reviews

We appreciate the help and input from everyone. In particular, we'd like to give the following people our special thanks:

Jader Franceschi, **Actúa Idiomas**, Bento Gonçalves, Rio Grande do Sul, Brazil

Juliana Dos Santos Voltan Costa, **Actus Idiomas**, São Paulo, Brazil

Ella Osorio, **Angelo State University**, San Angelo, TX, US

Mary Hunter, **Angelo State University**, San Angelo, TX, US

Mario César González, **Angloamericano de Monterrey, SC,** Monterrey, Mexico

Samantha Shipman, **Auburn High School**, Auburn, AL, US

Linda, **Bernick Language School**, Radford, VA, US

Dave Lowrance, **Bethesda University of California**, Yorba Linda, CA, US

Tajbakhsh Hosseini, **Bezmialem Vakif University**, Istanbul, Turkey

Dilek Gercek, **Bil English**, Izmir, Turkey

Erkan Kolat, **Biruni University, ELT**, Istanbul, Turkey

Nika Gutkowska, **Bluedata International**, New York, NY, US

Daniel Alcocer Gómez, **Cecati 92**, Guadalupe, Nuevo León, Mexico

Samantha Webb, **Central Middle School**, Milton-Freewater, OR, US

Verónica Salgado, **Centro Anglo Americano**, Cuernavaca, Mexico

Ana Rivadeneira Martínez and Georgia P. de Machuca, **Centro de Educación Continua – Universidad Politécnica del Ecuador,** Quito, Ecuador

Anderson Francisco Guimerães Maia, **Centro Cultural Brasil Estados Unidos**, Belém, Brazil

Rosana Mariano, **Centro Paula Souza**, São Paulo, Brazil

Carlos de la Paz Arroyo, Teresa Noemí Parra Alarcón, Gilberto Bastida Gaytan, Manuel Esquivel Román, and Rosa Cepeda Tapia, **Centro Universitario Angloamericano,** Cuernavaca, Morelos, Mexico

Antonio Almeida, **CETEC**, Morelos, Mexico

Cinthia Ferreira, **Cinthia Ferreira Languages Services,** Toronto, ON, Canada

Phil Thomas and Sérgio Sanchez, **CLS Canadian Language School,** São Paulo, Brazil

Celia Concannon, **Cochise College**, Nogales, AZ, US

Maria do Carmo Rocha and CAOP English team, **Colégio Arquidiocesano Ouro Preto – Unidade Cônego Paulo Dilascio,** Ouro Preto, Brazil

Kim Rodriguez, **College of Charleston North**, Charleston, SC, US

Jesús Leza Alvarado, **Coparmex English Institute,** Monterrey, Mexico

John Partain, **Cortazar**, Guanajuato, Mexico

Alexander Palencia Navas, **Cursos de Lenguas, Universidad del Atlántico**, Barranquilla, Colombia

Kenneth Johan Gerardo Steenhuisen Cera, Melfi Osvaldo Guzman Triana, and Carlos Alberto Algarín Jiminez, **Cursos de Lenguas Extranjeras Universidad del Atlantico,** Barranquilla, Colombia

Jane P Kerford, **East Los Angeles College**, Pasadena, CA, US

Daniela, **East Village**, Campinas, São Paulo, Brazil

Rosalva Camacho Orduño, **Easy English for Groups S.A. de C.V.**, Monterrey, Nuevo León, Mexico

Adonis Gimenez Fusetti, **Easy Way Idiomas**, Ibiúna, Brazil

Eileen Thompson, **Edison Community College**, Piqua, OH, US

Ahminne Handeri O.L Froede, **Englishouse escola de idiomas,** Teófilo Otoni, Brazil

Ana Luz Delgado-Izazola, **Escuela Nacional Preparatoria 5, UNAM,** Mexico City, Mexico

Nancy Alarcón Mendoza, **Facultad de Estudios Superiores Zaragoza, UNAM,** Mexico City, Mexico

Marcilio N. Barros, **Fast English USA**, Campinas, São Paulo, Brazil

Greta Douthat, **FCI Ashland**, Ashland, KY, US

Carlos Lizárraga González, **Grupo Educativo Anglo Americano, S.C.,** Mexico City, Mexico

Hugo Fernando Alcántar Valle, **Instituto Politécnico Nacional, Escuela Superior de Comercio y Administración-Unidad Santotomás, Celex Esca Santo Tomás,** Mexico City, Mexico

Sueli Nascimento, **Instituto Superior de Educação do Rio de Janeiro,** Rio de Janeiro, Brazil

Elsa F Monteverde, **International Academic Services,** Miami, FL, US

Laura Anand, **Irvine Adult School**, Irvine, CA, US

Prof. Marli T. Fernandes (principal) and Prof. Dr. Jefferson J. Fernandes (pedagogue), **Jefferson Idiomas**, São Paulo, Brazil

Herman Bartelen, **Kanda Gaigo Gakuin**, Tokyo, Japan

Cassia Silva, **Key Languages**, Key Biscayne, FL, US

Sister Mary Hope, **Kyoto Notre Dame Joshi Gakuin**, Kyoto, Japan

Nate Freedman, **LAL Language Centres**, Boston, MA, US

Richard Janzen, **Langley Secondary School**, Abbotsford, BC, Canada

Christina Abel Gabardo, **Language House,** Campo Largo, Brazil

Ivonne Castro, **Learn English International,** Cali, Colombia

Julio Cesar Maciel Rodrigues, **Liberty Centro de Línguas,** São Paulo, Brazil

Ann Gibson, **Maynard High School,** Maynard, MA, US

Martin Darling, **Meiji Gakuin Daigaku,** Tokyo, Japan

Dax Thomas, **Meiji Gakuin Daigaku,** Yokohama, Kanagawa, Japan

Derya Budak, **Mevlana University,** Konya, Turkey

B Sullivan, **Miami Valley Career Technical Center International Program,** Dayton, OH, US

Julio Velazquez, **Milo Language Center,** Weston, FL, US

Daiane Siqueira da Silva, Luiz Carlos Buontempo, Marlete Avelina de Oliveira Cunha, Marcos Paulo Segatti, Morgana Eveline de Oliveira, Nadia Lia Gino Alo, and Paul Hyde Budgen, **New Interchange-Escola de Idiomas,** São Paulo, Brazil

Patrícia França Furtado da Costa, Juiz de Fora, Brazil

Patricia Servín

Chris Pollard, **North West Regional College SK,** North Battleford, SK, Canada

Olga Amy, **Notre Dame High School,** Red Deer, Canada

Amy Garrett, **Ouachita Baptist University,** Arkadelphia, AR, US

Mervin Curry, **Palm Beach State College,** Boca Raton, FL, US

Julie Barros, **Quality English Studio,** Guarulhos, São Paulo, Brazil

Teodoro González Saldaña and Jesús Monserrrta Mata Franco, **Race Idiomas,** Mexico City, Mexico

Autumn Westphal and Noga La`or, **Rennert International,** New York, NY, US

Antonio Gallo and Javy Palau, **Rigby Idiomas,** Monterrey, Mexico Tatiane Gabriela Sperb do Nascimento, **Right Way,** Igrejinha, Brazil

Mustafa Akgül, **Selahaddin Eyyubi Universitesi,** Diyarbakır, Turkey

James Drury M. Fonseca, **Senac Idiomas Fortaleza,** Fortaleza, Ceara, Brazil

Manoel Fialho S Neto, **Senac – PE,** Recife, Brazil

Jane Imber, **Small World,** Lawrence, KS, US

Tony Torres, **South Texas College,** McAllen, TX, US

Janet Rose, **Tennessee Foreign Language Institute,** College Grove, TN, US

Todd Enslen, **Tohoku University,** Sendai, Miyagi, Japan

Daniel Murray, **Torrance Adult School,** Torrance, CA, US

Juan Manuel Pulido Mendoza, **Universidad del Atlántico,** Barranquilla, Colombia

Juan Carlos Vargas Millán, **Universidad Libre Seccional Cali,** Cali (Valle del Cauca), Colombia

Carmen Cecilia Llanos Ospina, **Universidad Libre Seccional Cali,** Cali, Colombia

Jorge Noriega Zenteno, **Universidad Politécnica del Valle de México,** Estado de México, Mexico

Aimee Natasha Holguin S., **Universidad Politécnica del Valle de México UPVM,** Tultitlàn Estado de México, Mexico

Christian Selene Bernal Barraza, **UPVM Universidad Politécnica del Valle de México,** Ecatepec, Mexico

Lizeth Ramos Acosta, **Universidad Santiago de Cali,** Cali, Colombia

Silvana Dushku, **University of Illinois Champaign,** IL, US

Deirdre McMurtry, **University of Nebraska – Omaha,** Omaha, NE, US

Jason E Mower, **University of Utah,** Salt Lake City, UT, US

Paul Chugg, **Vanguard Taylor Language Institute,** Edmonton, Alberta, Canada

Henry Mulak, **Varsity Tutors,** Los Angeles, CA, US

Shirlei Strucker Calgaro and Hugo Guilherme Karrer, **VIP Centro de Idiomas,** Panambi, Rio Grande do Sul, Brazil

Eleanor Kelly, **Waseda Daigaku Extension Centre,** Tokyo, Japan

Sherry Ashworth, **Wichita State University,** Wichita, KS, US

Laine Bourdene, **William Carey University,** Hattiesburg, MS, US

Serap Aydın, Istanbul, Turkey

Liliana Covino, Guarulhos, Brazil

Yannuarys Jiménez, Barranquilla, Colombia

Juliana Morais Pazzini, Toronto, ON, Canada

Marlon Sanches, Montreal, Canada

Additional content contributed by Kenna Bourke, Inara Couto, Nic Harris, Greg Manin, Ashleigh Martinez, Laura McKenzie, Paul McIntyre, Clara Prado, Lynne Robertson, Mari Vargo, Theo Walker, and Maria Lucia Zaorob.

Plan of Book 2B

Pronunciation/Listening	Writing/Reading	Interchange Activity
Intonation in statements with time phrases Listening to people talk about changes	Writing a paragraph describing a person's past, present, and possible future "Aquaviva: Fighting for a Future": Reading about a town's attempt to attract new residents	"Cause and effect": Agreeing and disagreeing with classmates **PAGE 123**
Unreleased and released /t/ and /d/ Listening to people talk about their job preferences	Writing a an online cover letter for a job application "Global Work Solutions": Reading about understanding cultural differences in an international company	"You're hired.": Interviewing for a job **PAGE 124**
The letter o Listening to descriptions of monuments; listening for information about a country	Writing an introduction to an online city guide Reading about unusual museums	"True or false?": Sharing information about famous works **PAGE 125**
Contrastive stress in responses Listening to stories about unexpected experiences	Writing a description of a recent experience "Breaking Down the Sound of Silence": Reading about an unusual rock band	"It's my life.": Playing a board game to share past experiences **PAGE 126**
Emphatic stress Listening for opinions; listening to a movie review	Writing a movie review "The Real Art of Acting": Reading about unpleasant experiences actors put themselves through	"It was hilarious!": Asking classmates' opinions about movies, TV shows, and celebrities **PAGE 127**
Pitch Listening to people talk about the meaning of signs	Writing a list of rules "Understanding Idioms": Reading about idioms and their meaning	"Casual observers": Interpreting body language **PAGE 128**
Reduction of *have* Listening to people talk about predicaments; listening to a call-in radio show	Writing a blog post asking for advice "TOPTIPS.COM": Reading an online advice forum	"Tough choices": Deciding what to do in a difficult situation **PAGE 130**
Reduction of *had* and *would* Listening for excuses	Writing a report about people's responses to a survey "A Good Excuse for a Day Off Work": Reading about taking a sick day	"Just a bunch of excuses": Discussing calendar conflicts and making up excuses **PAGES 129, 131**

9 Only time will tell.

▸ **Discuss life in different times**
▸ **Discuss consequences**

1 SNAPSHOT

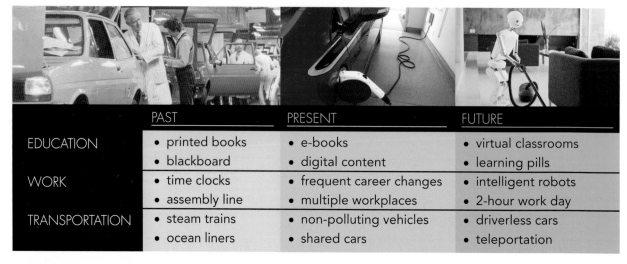

	PAST	PRESENT	FUTURE
EDUCATION	• printed books • blackboard	• e-books • digital content	• virtual classrooms • learning pills
WORK	• time clocks • assembly line	• frequent career changes • multiple workplaces	• intelligent robots • 2-hour work day
TRANSPORTATION	• steam trains • ocean liners	• non-polluting vehicles • shared cars	• driverless cars • teleportation

Which of these changes are the most important? How have they affected the way we live?
Do you think any of the future developments could happen in your lifetime?
Can you think of two other developments that could happen in the future?

2 CONVERSATION That's a thing of the past!

▸ **A** Listen and practice.

Tom: I hardly recognize our old neighborhood. A few years ago, there were just houses around here.

Mia: I know. They're building a lot of new apartments. The whole neighborhood's different.

Tom: Remember the little burger restaurant we used to go to after school, Hamburger Heaven?

Mia: Of course . . . Now it's another office tower. And I hear they're tearing down our high school. They're going to build a shopping mall.

Tom: That's such a shame. Pretty soon the neighborhood will just be a bunch of malls. And maybe there won't be any schools anymore.

Mia: Probably not. Kids will study from their computers anywhere they want.

Tom: So they won't hang out with their friends after school? That's too bad. I enjoyed meeting our friends at that burger place after class.

Mia: Seriously? That's a thing of the past! Nowadays, kids only meet online.

▸ **B** Listen to the rest of the conversation. What else has changed in their neighborhood?

3 GRAMMAR FOCUS

Time contrasts

Past	Present	Future
A few years ago, there **were** just houses here.	These days, they**'re building** lots of apartments.	Soon, there **will be** apartment blocks everywhere.
We **used to go** to a burger place after class every day.	Today, people **order** food from their phones.	In the future, restaurants **might not exist**.
In the past, kids **used to hang out** with friends after school.	Nowadays, kids only **meet** online.	In a few years, we **are going to have** virtual friends.

GRAMMAR PLUS *see page 140*

A Complete the sentences in column A with the appropriate information from column B. Then compare with a partner.

A

1. In the early 1990s, ___
2. Before the airplane, ___
3. Before there were supermarkets, ___
4. In many companies these days, ___
5. In most big cities nowadays, ___
6. In many schools today, ___
7. In the next 100 years, ___
8. Sometime in the near future, ___

B

a. students have their own tablets.
b. pollution is becoming a serious problem.
c. there will probably be cities in space.
d. few people had cell phones.
e. people used to shop at small grocery stores.
f. women still receive lower salaries than men.
g. doctors might find a cure for the common cold.
h. ocean liners were the only way to travel across the Atlantic.

B Complete four of the phrases in part A, column A, with your own ideas. Then compare with a partner.

4 PRONUNCIATION Intonation in statements with time phrases

A Listen and practice. Notice the intonation in these statements beginning with a time phrase.

In the past, few women went to college.

Today, there are more women than men in college in the United States.

In the future, women all over the world will go to college.

B **PAIR WORK** Complete these statements with your own information. Then read your statements to a partner. Pay attention to intonation.

As a child, I used to . . .   These days, . . .

Five years ago, I . . .   In five years, I'll . . .

Nowadays, I . . .   In ten years, I might . . .

5 LISTENING On the other side of the world

▶ **A** Listen to Katie talk to her grandfather about an upcoming trip. Check (✓) the three concerns her grandfather has about the trip.

Concern

Katie's response

1. ☐ language   ☐ transportation   _____
2. ☐ meeting people ☐ money   _____
3. ☐ communication ☐ food   _____

▶ **B** Listen again. Write what Katie says in response to these concerns.

C **PAIR WORK** What other problems might someone experience when they travel to another country? How might these problems change in the future?

6 SPEAKING Not anymore.

GROUP WORK How have things changed? How will things be different in the future? Choose four of these topics. Then discuss the questions below.

communications	education	housing
entertainment	fashion	shopping
environment	food	traveling
health		

What was it like in the past?
What is it like today?
What will it be like in the future?

A: In the past, people cooked all their meals at home.
B: Not anymore. Nowadays, we eat takeout food all the time.
C: In the future, . . .

7 WRITING He's changed a lot.

A **PAIR WORK** Interview your partner about his or her past, present, and hopes for the future.

B Write a paragraph describing how your partner has changed. Make some predictions about the future. Don't write your partner's name.

> This person came to our school about two years ago. He used to be a little shy in class, and he didn't have many friends. Now, he's on the basketball team and he is very popular. He's a very talented player and, someday, he'll play on the national team. He'll be famous and very rich. I think he'll . . .

C **CLASS ACTIVITY** Read your paragraph to the class. Can they guess who it is about?

8 PERSPECTIVES Making the big bucks

▶ **A** Listen to some possible consequences of getting a high-paying job.
Check (✓) the statements you agree with.

If you get a high-paying job, . . .

☐ your friends might ask you for a loan.

☐ you'll have a lot of money to spend.

☐ more people may want to be your friend.

☐ you won't have much time for your family.

☐ you'll be able to buy anything you want.

☐ you won't be able to take long vacations.

☐ you'll have to pay higher taxes.

☐ you won't have to worry about the future.

B **PAIR WORK** Look at the statements again. Which are advantages
of getting a high-paying job? Which are disadvantages?

"The first one is a disadvantage. I'd like to help my friends, but I wouldn't
like to lend them money."

9 GRAMMAR FOCUS

▶ **Conditional sentences with *if* clauses**

Possible situation (present)	Consequence (future with *will*, *may*, or *might*)
If you **get** a high-paying job,	you**'ll have** more cash to spend.
If you **have** more cash to spend,	you**'ll be able to buy** anything you want.
If you **can buy** anything you want,	you **won't save** your money.
If you **don't save** your money,	you **may have to get** a weekend job.
If you **have to get** a weekend job,	you **might not have** any free time.

GRAMMAR PLUS *see page 140*

A Match the *if* clauses in column A with the appropriate consequences from column B. Then compare
with a partner.

A

1. If you eat less fast food, ____
2. If you walk to work every day, ____
3. If you don't get enough sleep, ____
4. If you change jobs, ____
5. If you don't study regularly, ____
6. If you travel abroad, ____

B

a. you may not learn to speak fluently.
b. you might feel a lot healthier.
c. you'll stay in shape without joining a gym.
d. you'll be able to experience a new culture.
e. you won't be able to stay awake in class.
f. you may not like it better than your old one.

B Add your own consequences to the *if* clauses in column A. Then practice with a partner.

"If you eat less fast food, you will probably live longer."

10 WORD POWER Collocations

A PAIR WORK Find phrases from the list that usually go with each verb.
(Sometimes more than one answer is possible.)

a club	a gym	in shape	money	tired
✓ a degree	a living	into college	stressed	work experience
a group	energy	jealous	time	your own money

earn   _a degree_   _____   _____

get   _____   _____   _____

join   _____   _____   _____

spend _____   _____   _____

feel   _____   _____   _____

B GROUP WORK Share your answers with the group.
Can you add one more phrase to each verb?

11 SPEAKING Who knows what will happen?

A GROUP WORK Choose three possible events from below. One student completes an event with a consequence. The next student adds a consequence. Suggest at least five consequences.

fall in love   get a part-time job

join a gym   move to a foreign country

study very hard

If you fall in love, you'll probably want to get married.

If you get married, you'll have to earn your own money.

If you want to earn your own money, you'll need to get a job.

If you get a job, you may spend less time at the gym.

If you spend less time at the gym, you won't keep in shape.

B CLASS ACTIVITY Who has the most interesting consequences for each event?

12 INTERCHANGE 9 Cause and effect

Give your opinion about some issues. Go to Interchange 9 on page 123.

A Scan the article. Where is Aguaviva? Who is Luis Bricio?

AGUAVIVA: FIGHTING FOR A FUTURE

Twenty years ago, Aguaviva, a small village in the north of Spain, was dying. Young people wanted more opportunities, so they moved away to the cities. By 1991, there were only 618 people left, and most of them were old. Many of the houses were empty and falling down, and the local school had very few children. Aguaviva's future looked dark.

In 2000, the mayor, Luis Bricio, decided something had to change. He wondered, "How can I bring this place back to life?" He knew the village needed people, but from where? Then he had a brilliant idea. He flew 6,300 miles to Buenos Aires and started telling everyone about Aguaviva. He spoke on the radio and put advertisements in newspapers. The ads said, "If you are married with two children under the age of 12, we'll offer you

a home, a job, free health care and education for at least five years." The following year, he did the same thing in Romania.

Many families accepted the offer and Aguaviva began to change. The village school went from having 37 students to more than 80 in three years. The sound of children shouting and playing has made the local people feel so much younger. The economy began to improve, too. There was work for builders repairing the old houses, and a factory making electrical parts for cars opened.

Of course, not everything was easy. The people from Buenos Aires were used to a big city, so living in a small village with little public transportation was difficult at first. The Romanians had to learn a new language. And they all missed their family and friends back home. But everybody had new opportunities, too. Before, many of the parents had worried about finding a job and having enough money to look after their children. After moving to Spain, their future looked brighter. Many of them thought, "We're going to stay here for many years – this place will be our home."

B Read the article. Then answer the questions.

1. Why did young people start leaving Aguaviva?
2. How did Luis Bricio try to attract people to Aguaviva?
3. How did the school change after the year 2000?
4. What kinds of new jobs were there in Aguaviva?
5. What problems did the families from Argentina and Romania have?

C Who would make the following comments? Choose the correct words from the box.

| Luis Bricio | young people from Aguaviva |
| elderly people from Aguaviva | new immigrants |

1. "I'm not going back home because life is better here." _____
2. "I can't stay here. There are no jobs for people of my age." _____
3. "I'm going to make this village a better place." _____
4. "I love having all these kids around me – I don't feel so old." _____

D Do you think Luis Bricio had a good idea? Would you move to a place like this? What would you miss most about home?

I like working with people.

▸ Discuss job skills
▸ Discuss kinds of jobs

1 SNAPSHOT

21ST CENTURY SKILLS

☐ Can you use technology to find the information you need?

☐ Can you evaluate the information you find?

☐ Do you work well with different kinds of people?

☐ Can you communicate with people from different cultures?

☐ Are you good at analyzing and solving problems?

☐ Can you develop new ideas?

☐ Do you enjoy learning new things?

☐ Can you teach others how to do things?

21st century life citizen skills creativity successful digital effective knowledge information responsibility network fluency flexibility technology effective collaborate ability thinking global critical

Which of these skills do you think are most important for work? in life? Why?

Check (✓) the skills that you think you have.

Look at the skills you checked. What jobs do you think you might be good at?

2 CONVERSATION I love playing video games.

▶ **A** Listen and practice.

Mai: What are you doing this summer?

Jeff: Nothing much. I'm broke. I need to find a job!

Mai: So do I. Have you seen anything interesting?

Jeff: No, not yet.

Mai: Why don't you get a job at your uncle's restaurant?

Jeff: No way. They're open evenings and weekends, and I hate working on weekends.

Mai: Well, I don't mind working on weekends. Besides, I really enjoy working with people. Do you think he would give me a job?

Jeff: Why don't you go over this weekend and talk to him?

Mai: Yeah. I'll do that. Oh, I found one for you: video game tester.

Jeff: That sounds like fun. I love playing video games. I'll check that one out.

▶ **B** Listen to the rest of the conversation. What is one problem with the job? What does Jeff decide to do?

Gerunds; short responses

Affirmative statements with gerunds	Agree	Disagree	Other verbs or phrases followed by gerunds
I love playing video games.	So do I.	I don't.	like + √ / √_ing
I hate working on weekends.	So do I.	Really? I like it.	enjoy + √_ing
I'm good at solving problems.	So am I.	Oh, I'm not.	be interested in
Negative statements with gerunds			
I don't mind working evenings.	Neither do I.	I do.	
I'm not good at selling.	Neither am I.	Well, I am.	
I can't stand commuting.	Neither can I.	Oh, I don't mind it.	

GRAMMAR PLUS *see page 141*

A PAIR WORK Match the phrases in columns A and B to make statements about yourself. Then take turns reading your sentences and giving short responses.

A
1. I can't stand ____
2. I'm not very good at ____
3. I'm good at ____
4. I don't like ____
5. I hate ____
6. I'm interested in ____
7. I don't mind ____
8. I enjoy ____

B
a. working the night shift.
b. solving other people's problems.
c. working alone.
d. sitting in long meetings.
e. working on weekends.
f. speaking in public.
g. managing my time.
h. learning foreign languages.

A: I can't stand sitting in long meetings.
B: Neither can I.

B GROUP WORK Complete the phrases in column A with your own information. Then take turns reading your statements. Ask questions to get more information.

4 PRONUNCIATION Unreleased and released /t/ and /d/

A Listen and practice. Notice that when the sound /t/ or /d/ at the end of a word is followed by a consonant, it's unreleased. When it is followed by a vowel sound, it's released.

Unreleased
She's not good at dealing with stress.
I hate working on Sundays.
You need to manage money well.

Released
He's not a good artist.
They really hate it!
I need a cup of coffee.

B PAIR WORK Write three sentences starting with *I'm not very good at* and *I don't mind*. Then practice the sentences. Pay attention to the unreleased and released sounds /t/ and /d/.

5 SPEAKING Do what you love.

A PAIR WORK How does your partner feel about doing these things? Interview your partner. Check (✓) his or her answers.

How do you feel about . . . ?	I enjoy it.	I don't mind it.	I hate it.
dealing with the public	☐	☐	☐
working alone	☐	☐	☐
being part of a team	☐	☐	☐
meeting deadlines	☐	☐	☐
leading a team	☐	☐	☐
working on weekends	☐	☐	☐
learning new skills	☐	☐	☐
doing the same thing every day	☐	☐	☐
traveling	☐	☐	☐
making decisions	☐	☐	☐
helping people	☐	☐	☐
solving problems	☐	☐	☐

B PAIR WORK Look back at the information in part A. Suggest a job for your partner.

A: You enjoy dealing with the public, and you hate working alone. You'd be a good salesperson.

B: But I hate working on weekends.

A: Maybe you could . . .

6 LISTENING My ideal career

▶ **A** Listen to people talk about the kind of work they are looking for. Then check (✓) each person's ideal job.

1. Alex
- ☑ architect
- ☐ accountant
- ☐ teacher

2. Evelyn
- ☐ banker
- ☑ doctor
- ☐ lawyer

3. Edward
- ☐ marine biologist
- ☐ songwriter
- ☑ flight attendant

▶ **B** Listen again. Write two reasons each person gives for his or her ideal job.

1. Alex _He's good a drawing_ _like to design at home_
2. Evelyn _help people in develop countries._ _go to medical school._
3. Edward _travelling_ _work in a team / with people_
   like

7 INTERCHANGE 10 You're hired.

Choose the right person for the job. Go to Interchange 10 on page 124.

8 WORD POWER Personality traits

A Which of these adjectives are positive (**P**)? Which are negative (**N**)?

creative	P	impatient	
critical		level-headed	
disorganized		moody	
efficient		punctual	
forgetful		reliable	
generous		short-tempered	
hardworking		strict	

disorganized

hardworking

B **PAIR WORK** Tell your partner about people you know with these personality traits.

"My boss is very short-tempered. She often shouts at people . . ."

C Listen to four conversations. Then check (✓) the adjective that best describes each person.

1. a boss
- [ ] creative
- [ ] forgetful
- [ ] serious

2. a co-worker
- [ ] unfriendly
- [ ] generous
- [ ] strange

3. a teacher
- [ ] moody
- [ ] patient
- [ ] hardworking

4. a relative
- [ ] short-tempered
- [ ] disorganized
- [ ] reliable

9 PERSPECTIVES Making the right choice

A Listen to these people answer the question, "What kind of work would you like to do?" What job does each person talk about? Do they want that job?

Paula

"Well, I think I'd make a good journalist because I'm good at writing. When I was in high school, I worked as a reporter for the school website. I really enjoyed writing different kinds of articles."

Shawn

"I know what I *don't* want to do! A lot of my friends work in the stock market, but I could never be a stockbroker because I can't make decisions quickly. I don't mind working hard, but I'm terrible under pressure!"

Dalia

"I'm still in school. My parents want me to be a teacher, but I'm not sure yet. I guess I could be a teacher because I'm very creative. I'm also very impatient, so maybe I shouldn't work with kids."

B **PAIR WORK** Look at the interviews again. Who are you most like? least like? Why?

> **Clauses with *because***
>
> **The word *because* introduces a cause or reason.**
>
> I'd make a good journalist **because I'm good at writing**.
>
> I could be a teacher **because I'm very creative**.
>
> I wouldn't want to be a teacher **because I'm very impatient**.
>
> I could never be a stockbroker **because I can't make decisions quickly**.
>
> **GRAMMAR PLUS** *see page 141*

A Complete the sentences in column A with appropriate information from column B. Then compare with a partner.

A	B
1. I'd like to be a physical therapist ____	**a.** because I'm very disorganized.
2. I would make a bad librarian ____	**b.** because I love animals.
3. I couldn't be a diplomat ____	**c.** because I enjoy helping people.
4. I wouldn't mind working as a veterinarian ____	**d.** because I'm not good at managing money.
5. I could be a flight attendant ____	**e.** because I'm short-tempered.
6. I could never be a financial advisor ____	**f.** because I really enjoy traveling.

B **GROUP WORK** Think about your personal qualities and skills. Then complete these statements. Take turns discussing them with your group.

I could never be a . . . because . . .   I'd make a good . . . because . . .

I wouldn't mind working as a . . . because . . .   The best job for me is . . . because . . .

11 WRITING An online cover letter for a job application

A Imagine you are applying for one of the jobs in this unit. Write a short cover letter for a job application.

Reply Forward

To: Catherine West

Subject: News reporter position – ref. 04532

Dear Ms. West,

I was excited to see your opening for a news reporter, and I hope to be invited for an interview. I think I could make a great addition to your team because I'm very hardworking, and I really enjoy writing.

As you can see from my résumé, I've had a lot of experience writing for my high school newspaper and for my college website. I also worked . . .

B **PAIR WORK** Exchange papers. If you received this cover letter, would you invite the applicant for a job interview? Why or why not?

A Skim the advertisement. Which three cross-cultural problems does it mention?

GLOBAL WORK SOLUTIONS

At GW Solutions, we recognize the importance of cross-cultural training for U.S. employees working abroad. Lack of cultural understanding results in lost contracts and less business. Here are some examples of what our courses can teach you.

In the U.S.A., we say that time is money. For American workers, punctuality and timetables are always important. At work, people concentrate on the task they are doing. They usually do not spend a lot of time on small talk. However, it's important to realize that not all cultures see time in this way. In many African countries, for example, getting work done isn't the only valuable use of time. Spending time at work to build close relationships with colleagues is equally important. It's important to ask about your colleague's personal life. Understanding these cultural differences is essential for working in a global team. If an American doesn't realize this, he or she might think that an African colleague who spends a lot of time chatting with co-workers is being lazy or avoiding doing his or her work. And an African worker might think their American colleague is the rudest person they've ever met!

In the U.S.A., written agreements are essential. Business deals are always agreed through a contract and once it has been signed, we consider it to be final. The conditions of the agreement don't usually change without the signing of another contract. But you may do business in places where this is not the case. In China, for example, people generally place more trust in a person's word than in a signed contract. Once a good relationship exists, a simple handshake might be enough to reach a business deal.

In the U.S.A., workers generally speak directly, and they openly disagree with colleagues. This kind of "straight talk" is seen as a mark of honesty. But where we see honesty, others may see rudeness. In some parts of Asia, open disagreement with colleagues may not be acceptable because it makes people feel embarrassed. Instead, you should stop and think for a while. Afterward you could say, "I agree in general, but could a different idea work in this situation?" And your body language is important, too. In the West, direct eye contact is good because it's a sign of honesty. In some Asian cultures, it's polite to avoid looking directly at your colleagues in order to show respect.

Did you learn something new? Need to know more? Sign up for one of our training courses and learn how to do business wherever you go.

B Read the advertisement. Then correct the sentences.

1. Ideas about work time are the same in Africa and the U.S.A.
2. Written contracts are more important in China than in the U.S.A.
3. American and Asian workers have similar ways of communicating.

C Complete these sentences with words from the advertisement.

1. In the U.S.A., being _____ is very important at work.
2. African workers like to have strong _____ with their co-workers.
3. In China, people might agree to a business deal with a _____.
4. For Americans, it's normal to _____ openly when they have a different opinion.
5. Some workers _____ making eye contact when talking to others.

D Look at the sentences in part C. Are they true for your country? What advice would you give to a foreigner coming to work in your country?

Units 9–10 Progress check

SELF-ASSESSMENT

How well can you do these things? Check (✓) the boxes.

I can . . .	Very well	OK	A little
Describe people and things in the past, present, and future (Ex. 1)	☐	☐	☐
Discuss possible consequences of actions (Ex. 2)	☐	☐	☐
Understand descriptions of skills and personality traits (Ex. 3, 4)	☐	☐	☐
Discuss job skills (Ex. 4)	☐	☐	☐
Give reasons for my opinions (Ex. 4)	☐	☐	☐

1 SPEAKING Things have changed.

A PAIR WORK Think of one more question for each category. Then interview a partner.

Free time How did you spend your free time as a child? What do you like to do these days? How are you going to spend your free time next year?

Friends Who used to be your friends when you were a kid? How do you meet new people nowadays? How do you think people will meet in the future?

B GROUP WORK Share one interesting thing about your partner.

2 GAME Share the consequences

A Add two situations and two consequences to the lists below.

Situation	Consequences
☐ you spend too much time online	☐ learn about a different culture
☐ you get a well-paid job	☐ get good grades
☐ you move to a foreign country	☐ buy an expensive car
☐ it's sunny tomorrow	☐ feel jealous sometimes
☐ you don't study hard	☐ go to the beach
☐ you fall in love	☐ have time for your family and friends
☐ _____	☐ _____
☐ _____	☐ _____

B CLASS ACTIVITY Go around the class and make sentences. Check (✓) each *if* clause after you use it. The student who uses the most clauses correctly wins.

"If you spend too much time online, you won't . . ."

3 LISTENING What do you want to do?

A Listen to Michelle and Robbie discuss four jobs. Write down the jobs and check (✓) if they would be good or bad at them.

	Job	Good	Bad	Reason
1. Michelle		☐ ☐	☐ ☐	
2. Robbie		☐ ☐	☐ ☐	

B Listen again. Write down the reasons they give.

C **PAIR WORK** Look at the jobs from part A. Which ones would you be good at? Why?

4 DISCUSSION Job profile

A Prepare a personal job profile. Write your name, skills, and job preferences. Think about the questions below. Then compare with a partner.

Do you . . . ?
enjoy helping people
have any special skills
have any experience
have a good memory

Are you good at . . . ?
communicating with people
solving problems
making decisions quickly
learning foreign languages

Do you mind . . . ?
wearing a uniform
traveling frequently
working with a team
working long hours

A: Do you enjoy helping people?
B: Sure. I often do volunteer work.
A: So do I. I help at our local . . .

B **GROUP WORK** Make suggestions for possible jobs based on your classmates' job profiles. Give reasons for your opinions. What do you think of their suggestions for you?

A: Victor would be a good psychologist because he's good at communicating with people.
B: No way! I could never be a psychologist. I'm very moody and short-tempered!

WHAT'S NEXT?

Look at your Self-assessment again. Do you need to review anything?

11 It's really worth seeing!

▶ **Discuss famous landmarks, monuments, and works of art**
▶ **Discuss countries around the world**

1 SNAPSHOT

AMAZING FACTS ABOUT AMAZING LANDMARKS

The Eiffel Tower – When it was opened in 1889, the tower was red. After a decade, it was painted yellow, and later, it was covered in different shades of brown.

Machu Picchu – It is located 2,430 m (7,972 ft) above sea level, and it has resisted several earthquakes. When there is an earthquake, the stones "dance" and fall back into place.

The Neuschwanstein Castle – This beautiful castle in Germany was the inspiration for the Walt Disney Magic Kingdom Sleeping Beauty Castle.

Mount Fuji – The highest mountain in Japan is made up of a few volcanoes. The last recorded eruption started in 1707.

Big Ben – The tower is named Elizabeth Tower. Big Ben is the name of the bell inside it.

The Statue of Liberty – The 350 pieces were made in France and then shipped to the United States.

Did you know these facts about the landmarks above? What else do you know about them?
Have you ever visited any of them? Which would you like to visit? Why?
Do you know any interesting facts about landmarks in your country?

2 PERSPECTIVES Where dreams come true

▶ **A** How much do you know about the Walt Disney Company and theme parks?
Find three mistakes in the statements below. Then listen and check your answers.

1. The Walt Disney Company was founded in 1923 in California by Walt Disney and his brother Roy.
2. Their most famous character, Donald Duck, first appeared in a movie in 1928.
3. The first Disney theme park, Disneyland, was opened in 1955 in New York and soon became an international attraction.
4. The official opening was broadcast live by the ABC television network.
5. In 1971, the company opened their second park, Disney World.
6. Some of their most popular parks in Florida include Magic Kingdom, Animal Kingdom, and Epcot Center.
7. In 1983, the company opened their first foreign park, London Disneyland. Later, theme parks were also opened in Paris, Hong Kong, and Shanghai.

B **GROUP WORK** Have you been to a Disney park? Which one?
How did you like it? Which one would you like to go to? Why?

3 GRAMMAR FOCUS

▶ **Passive with *by* (simple past)**

The passive changes the focus of a sentence.

For the simple past, use the past of *be* + past participle.

Active	Passive
The Disney brothers **founded** the company in 1923.	It **was founded by** the Disney brothers in 1923.
Walt Disney **opened** Disneyland in 1955.	Disneyland **was opened by** Walt Disney in 1955.
The ABC network **broadcast** the opening of the park.	The opening **was broadcast by** ABC.

GRAMMAR PLUS *see page 142*

A Complete the sentences with the simple past passive form of the verbs. Then compare with a partner.

1. *Mont Sainte-Victoire* _____ (paint) by the French artist Paul Cézanne.
2. The first Star Wars film _____ (write) and _____ (direct) by George Lucas.
3. The Statue of Liberty _____ (design) by the French sculptor Frédéric Auguste Bartholdi.
4. The 2014 World Cup final _____ (win) by Germany. The final match _____ (see) by almost 1 billion people all over the world.
5. The songs *Revolution* and *Hey Jude* _____ (record) by the Beatles in 1968.
6. In the 2007 film *I'm Not There*, the American musician Bob Dylan _____ (play) by six different people, including Australian actress Cate Blanchett.
7. The 2016 Oscar for Best Actress _____ (give) to Brie Larson for her role in the movie *Room*.
8. The first iPad _____ (release) in 2010.

B PAIR WORK Change these sentences into passive sentences with *by*. Then take turns reading them aloud.

1. Eddie Redmayne played Stephen Hawking in the 2014 film *The Theory of Everything*.

   _____

2. Gabriel García Márquez wrote the novel *One Hundred Years of Solitude* in 1967.

   _____

3. The American architect William Lamb designed the Empire State Building.

   _____

4. Woo Paik produced the first digital HDTV in 1991.

   _____

5. J. K. Rowling wrote the first Harry Potter book on an old manual typewriter.

   _____

6. *Empire* magazine readers chose Indiana Jones as the greatest movie character of all time.

   _____

4 INTERCHANGE 11 True or false?

Who created these well-known works? Go to Interchange 11 on page 125.

5 PRONUNCIATION The letter o

▶ **A** Listen and practice. Notice how the letter o is pronounced in the following words.

/a/	/ou/	/u/	/ʌ/
not	no	do	one
top	don't	food	love
_____	_____	_____	_____
_____	_____	_____	_____

▶ **B** How is the letter o pronounced in these words? Write them in the correct column in part A. Then listen and check your answers.

come   done   lock   own   shot   soon   who   wrote

6 LISTENING Man-made wonders of the world

▶ **A** Listen to three tour guides describe some famous monuments.
Take notes to answer the questions below. Then compare with a partner.

1. Taj Mahal
Why was it built?
What do the changing colors of the building represent?

2. Palace of Versailles
What did King Louis XIV want the Hall of Mirrors to show?
What problem did the candles cause? How did the mirrors help?

3. La Sagrada Familia
What did the architect think about man-made structures versus nature?
Why are no straight lines used?

B PAIR WORK Think of another famous monument. Describe it to the rest of the class.
They will try to guess the monument.

7 WORD POWER Country fast facts

A Complete the sentences with words from the list.

✓ cattle	dialects	electronics	handicrafts	languages
sheep	souvenirs	✓ soybeans	textiles	wheat

1. The United States **grows** ___soybeans___ and _____.
2. Australia **raises** _____cattle_____ and _____.
3. China **manufactures** _____ and _____.
4. In India, people **speak** many different _____ and _____.
5. You can **find** _____ and _____ at different shops in Brazil.

B PAIR WORK Talk about your country. Use the sentences in part A with your own information.

"We raise cattle and chickens. We grow corn and oats. You can find . . . "

8 CONVERSATION What do you want to know?

▶ **A** Listen and practice.

Lisa: Erik, you're from Amsterdam, aren't you?

Erik: Yeah . . . Why?

Lisa: I'm going there for a conference, and I'd like some information.

Erik: Sure. What do you want to know?

Lisa: Do you use the euro in the Netherlands?

Erik: Yes. The euro is used in most of Europe, you know.

Lisa: And do I need to take euros with me?

Erik: Not really. International credit cards are accepted everywhere, and they're much safer.

Lisa: Of course. And what should I buy there?

Erik: Cheese, definitely. We raise dairy cows, and some really excellent cheese is made from their milk.

Lisa: Good. I love cheese. Where is it sold?

Erik: You can find it at cheese shops all around the city. And don't forget to bring me a piece.

NORTH SEA

AMSTERDAM

GERMANY

BELGIUM

▶ **B** Listen to the rest of the conversation. What other suggestion does Erik give Lisa?

9 GRAMMAR FOCUS

▶ **Passive without *by* (simple present)**

For the simple present, use the present of *be* + past participle.

Active	Passive
They **use** the euro in most of Europe.	The euro **is used** in most of Europe.
Most places **accept** credit cards.	Credit cards **are accepted** at most places.
We **raise** dairy cattle in the Netherlands.	Dairy cattle **are raised** in the Netherlands.

GRAMMAR PLUS *see page 142*

A Complete the sentences. Use the passive of these verbs.

grow   manufacture   raise   speak   sell   use

1. French and Flemish _____ in Belgium.
2. Rice _____ in many Asian countries.
3. Cars and electronics _____ in Japan.
4. Sheep's milk _____ for making feta cheese.
5. Handicrafts _____ in the streets in Thailand.
6. A lot of cattle _____ in Australia.

B Complete this passage using the simple present passive form.

Many crops _____ (grow) in Taiwan. Some crops _____ (consume) locally, but others _____ (export). Tea _____ (grow) in cooler parts of the island, and rice _____ (cultivate) in warmer parts. Fishing is also an important industry. A wide variety of seafood _____ (catch) and _____ (ship) all over the world. Many people _____ (employ) in the food-processing industry.

C **PAIR WORK** Use the passive of the verbs in part A to talk about your country and other countries you know.

10 LISTENING Is all tourism good?

▶ **A** Listen to a news report about tourism in Costa Rica. Select the six effects of mass tourism that are mentioned. (There are two extra effects.) Indicate if they are positive (**P**) or negative (**N**).

Costa Rica

P English is spoken.	The ocean is polluted.
Tourism jobs are available all over the country.	High-rise hotels are built.
More foreigners are investing there.	Fish and lobster are hunted.
Acres of jungle are cut down.	The government becomes corrupt.

▶ **B** Listen again. Write down three criteria the hotel fulfills in order to be an ecotourism business in Costa Rica.

_____   _____   _____

C **GROUP WORK** What is tourism like in your country? Talk about some positive and negative aspects.

11 SPEAKING Give me a clue.

A **PAIR WORK** Choose a country. Then answer these questions.

Where is it located?

What traditional dishes are eaten there?

What languages are spoken?

What currency is used?

What famous tourist attraction is found there?

What souvenirs are found there?

B **CLASS ACTIVITY** Give a short talk about the country you chose. Don't say the country's name. Can the class guess the country?

12 WRITING A city guide

A Choose a city or area in your country and write the introduction for an online city guide. Include the location, size, population, main attractions, shopping and travel tips, etc.

> Bruges is located in the northwest of Belgium, and it has a population of about 120,000 people. It is known for its canals and medieval buildings. In 2000, it was declared a World Heritage City by UNESCO. Bruges is also a good place to buy Belgium chocolate. It is sold . . .

Bruges, Belgium

B **GROUP WORK** Exchange papers. Do you think the introduction gives a good idea of the place? Would it attract tourists or businesses to the place? What other information should be included?

A Scan the advertisements. How many types of toilets can you see at the museum? When were the underwater sculptures designed? How big is the world's smallest book?

A SULABH INTERNATIONAL MUSEUM OF TOILETS, NEW DELHI, INDIA

Ever wondered about the history of toilets? Probably not! But visit the fascinating Sulabh Museum and see just how interesting they can be. Admire nearly 300 different toilets dating back to 2500 B.C.E. Some are beautifully decorated, one is made of solid gold, and there is an electric toilet that works without water. The star of the collection is a copy of a 16th century toilet. It was used by King Louis XIV of France – sometimes while speaking to his government. See drawings, photographs, and poems about toilets, too. One photo shows a toilet that was used by an elephant!

B UNDERWATER MUSEUM, CANCUN, MEXICO

Join one of our unique tours and discover an amazing underwater world 27 feet below the sea. Designed by Jason deCaires Taylor in 2009, it has over 450 sculptures. They are made from natural materials and show art and nature existing side by side. The *Silent Evolution* shows men, women, and children standing together on the seabed. They look so real that you'll want to talk to them. There are also sculptures of a house and a life-size Beetle car. The sculptures are covered in beautiful corals, and their appearances are constantly changing. Watch as an incredible variety of fish swim in and out of them.

C MICROMINIATURE MUSEUM, KIEV, UKRAINE

Small really is beautiful in this museum of art with a difference. The exhibits, created by artist Nikolai Syadristy, are so tiny they can only be seen clearly with a microscope. Read the world's smallest book – it is only 0.6 millimeters in size, but contains twelve pages of poems and drawings. There is a chess set on the head of a pin and the world's smallest electric motor. It is 20 times smaller than a piece of sand. Look closely at the eye of a needle and discover the seven camels inside. Read the words "Long Live Peace" not on paper, but written on a human hair!

B Read the advertisements. Find the words in *italics* below. Then circle the meaning of each word.

1. Something *fascinating* makes you feel very **interested / angry**.
2. The *star* of a collection is the **worst / best** part.
3. A *unique* thing is **different from / the same as** all others.
4. If something is changing *constantly*, it's changing **very little / all the time**.
5. An *exhibit* is an object that is **on show / for sale**.
6. A *needle* is a metal object that is used for **cutting / sewing**.

C Read the comments of three visitors to the museums. Write the letter (A, B, or C) of the museum you think they visited.

_____ **1.** "I just don't know how he made such little things."

_____ **2.** "I can't believe that an animal would use something like that."

_____ **3.** "I felt a little afraid about going down, but it was a great experience in the end."

D Which museum would you most like to visit? Why?

It's a long story.

▸ **Tell stories**
▸ **Discuss recent activities**

1 SNAPSHOT

True Stories of Incredible Coincidences

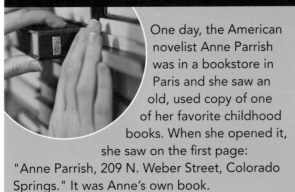

One day, the American novelist Anne Parrish was in a bookstore in Paris and she saw an old, used copy of one of her favorite childhood books. When she opened it, she saw on the first page: "Anne Parrish, 209 N. Weber Street, Colorado Springs." It was Anne's own book.

A 10-year-old girl named Laura Buxton released a bunch of balloons into the air. She attached a note to the balloons that asked the person who found it to write back to her. A couple of weeks later, she received a reply. It was from another 10-year-old girl also named Laura Buxton who lived 150 miles away.

Which of these stories do you think is more amazing? more difficult to believe?
Have you ever had an experience that is hard to believe?
Do you know of anyone who has? What happened?

2 PERSPECTIVES What next?

▶ **A** Listen to what happened to these people. Check (✓) the things that have happened to you.

- ☐ "I was having lunch when I spilled a cup of coffee on my clothes."
- ☐ "I was driving to the airport to pick up a friend, but I got a flat tire."
- ☐ "I was studying for an important test when the lights went out."
- ☐ "While I was walking down the street, I found a wallet with lots of money."
- ☐ "I was traveling in another country when I met an old school friend."
- ☐ "I was getting off a bus when I slipped and fell on the sidewalk."
- ☐ "While I was shopping one day, a celebrity walked into the store."

B Choose one statement that you checked. What happened next?

"I tried to clean it, but I couldn't. So I had to wear a jacket for the rest of the day."

▶ **Past continuous vs. simple past**

Use the past continuous for an action in progress in the past.
Use the simple past for an action that interrupts it.

I **was having** lunch	when I **spilled** coffee on my clothes.
I **was driving** to the airport,	but I **got** a flat tire.
While I **was shopping** one day,	a celebrity **walked** into the store.

GRAMMAR PLUS *see page 143*

A Complete these sentences. Then compare with a partner.

1. My sister _____ (text) while she _____ (drive), and she almost _____ (crash) her car.

2. While I _____ (cook) dinner last night, a friend _____ (call) and I _____ (burn) the food.

3. My father _____ (ski) when he _____ (break) his leg in several places.

4. We _____ (have) our first child while we _____ (live) in a tiny apartment.

5. While I _____ (drive) in England a few years ago, I _____ (realize) I was on the wrong side of the road!

6. Once I _____ (read) a good book, but someone _____ (tell) me the ending.

7. My parents _____ (meet) each other while they _____ (work) at the same restaurant in Vancouver.

B Complete these statements with information about yourself. Use the simple past or the past continuous.

1. I was taking a selfie when . . .
2. While I was going home one day, . . .
3. I was . . .
4. While I was . . .
5. Last month, . . .
6. Some time ago, . . .

C **PAIR WORK** Take turns reading your sentences from part B. Then ask and answer follow-up questions.

A: I was taking a selfie when a man came and stole my phone.
B: Oh, no! What did you do?
A: I went to the police . . . and they told me to be more careful.

4 LISTENING How did it all begin?

▶ **A** Listen to this story about a successful inventor. Put the sentences into the correct order from 1 to 8.

_1_ Mark Zuckerberg started writing computer programs.

____ His friends invested in Facebook.

____ He didn't accept Microsoft's offer.

____ He invented FaceMash.

____ Facebook became available to the public.

____ Zuckerberg wrote his very own messenger program.

____ He created a program that recommended music.

____ Three classmates asked for his help.

▶ **B** Listen again. How did the invention change his life?

C PAIR WORK Think of other websites and apps that were successful inventions.

5 WORD POWER What happened?

A Some adverbs are often used in storytelling to emphasize that something interesting is about to happen. Which of these adverbs are positive (**P**)? Which are negative (**N**)? Which could be either (**E**)?

coincidentally	____	strangely	____
fortunately	____	suddenly	____
luckily	____	surprisingly	____
miraculously	____	unexpectedly	____
sadly	____	unfortunately	____

B PAIR WORK Complete these statements with adverbs from part A to make up creative sentences.

We were having a party when, . . .
I was walking down the street when, . . .
It started out as a normal day, but, . . .

A: We were having a party when, suddenly, the lights went out!

B: Once I was dancing at a party when, unfortunately, I fell down!

6 WRITING What's your story?

A Write a short story about something that happened to you recently. Try to include some of the adverbs from Exercise 5.

> I was shopping at a big department store when, suddenly, I saw a little girl crying in a corner all by herself. The girl said she couldn't find her mother. I was taking her to the store manager when I saw an old school friend running towards me. Coincidentally, she was the girl's mother, and . . .

B GROUP WORK Take turns reading your stories. Answer any questions from the group.

7 CONVERSATION What have you been doing?

▶ **A** Listen and practice.

Steve: Hey, Luiza! I haven't seen you in ages. What have you been doing lately?

Luiza: I haven't been going out much. I've been working two jobs for the last six months.

Steve: How come?

Luiza: I'm saving up money for a trip to Morocco.

Steve: Well, that's exciting!

Luiza: Yeah, it is. What about you?

Steve: Well, I've only been *spending* money. I've been trying to become an actor. I've been taking courses and going to a lot of auditions.

Luiza: Really? How long have you been trying?

Steve: Since I graduated. But I haven't had any luck yet. No one recognizes my talent.

▶ **B** Listen to two other people at the party. What has happened since they last saw each other?

8 GRAMMAR FOCUS

▶ **Present perfect continuous**

Use the present perfect continuous for actions that start in the past and continue into the present.

What **have** you **been doing** lately?	I**'ve been working** two jobs for the last six months.
How long **have** you **been trying**?	I**'ve been trying** since I graduated.
Have you **been saving** money?	No, I **haven't been saving** money. I**'ve been spending** it!

GRAMMAR PLUS *see page 143*

A Complete the conversations with the present perfect continuous.

1. **A:** _____ you _____ (learn) any new skills this year?
   B: Yes, I have. I _____ (take) some art courses.

2. **A:** What _____ you _____ (do) lately?
   B: Well, I _____ (look for) a new job.

3. **A:** How _____ you _____ (feel) recently?
   B: Great! I _____ (run) three times a week. And I _____ (not drink) as much coffee since I stopped working at the coffee shop.

4. **A:** _____ you _____ (get) enough exercise lately?
   B: No, I haven't. I _____ (study) a lot for a big exam.

B **PAIR WORK** Read the conversations in part A together. Then read them again and answer the questions with your own information.

A: Have you been learning any new skills this year?
B: Yes, I've been taking guitar lessons.

It's a long story. **81**

9 PRONUNCIATION Contrastive stress in responses

▶ **A** Listen and practice. Notice how the stress changes to emphasize a contrast.

A: Has your brother been studying German?

B: No, I've been studying German.

A: Have you been teaching French?

B: No, I've been studying French.

▶ **B** Mark the stress changes in these conversations. Listen and check. Then practice the conversations.

A: Have you been studying for ten years?

B: No, I've been studying for two years.

A: Have you been studying at school?

B: No, I've been studying at home.

10 SPEAKING Tell me about it.

GROUP WORK Add three questions to this list. Then take turns asking and answering the questions. Remember to ask for further information.

Have you been . . . lately?

traveling

watching any good TV series

taking any lessons

working out

working long hours

going out a lot

staying up late

_____

_____

_____

useful expressions
Really?
I didn't know that!
Oh, I see.
I had no idea.
Wow! Tell me more.

A: Have you been traveling lately?

B: Yes, I have. I've been going abroad about once a month.

C: Really? Lucky you!

B: Not exactly. I've been traveling for work, not on vacation.

11 INTERCHANGE 12 It's my life.

Play a board game. Go to Interchange 12 on page 126.

A Skim the article. What is special about these musicians? How have they influenced other people?

BREAKING DOWN THE SOUND OF SILENCE

Ten years before he died, the composer Beethoven went deaf. He called this disability his "nightmare." Fortunately for thousands of classical music fans, he didn't stop writing brilliant music. One hundred and eighty years later, being deaf hasn't stopped three Americans – Steve Longo, Ed Chevy, and Bob Hiltermann – from playing music, either. In their case, the music is rock, and their band is called Beethoven's Nightmare.

The three boys grew up in different cities, but they all showed a surprising interest in music. Although they couldn't hear it, they were amazed by the energy of 1960s bands like the Beatles. They could see the effect the music had on the audiences – the happy faces of friends and family as they watched. Something exciting was obviously happening. "I'm going to do that, too," they all said. "Why? You can't hear," asked parents, teachers, and friends alike. Each boy used sign language to answer, "Because I can feel it."

Longo and Chevy started playing the guitar. They put on headphones and turned up the volume. With the help of powerful hearing aids, they could get some of the notes – the rest they felt through vibrations. Drummer Hiltermann came from a musical family. His parents thought that teaching their son to play an instrument was a waste of time. But they changed their minds after he nearly drove them crazy by using knives and forks to drum on the furniture of the house.

The three men first met in college in Washington, D.C. They started a band and played many concerts until they graduated in 1975. In 2001, Hiltermann had the idea to bring his old friends together again. They have been performing ever since. In 2013, a new member, Paul Raci, joined the band as a singer. At concerts, dancers put on a spectacular show and use sign language to explain the words of the songs to the audience. And, of course, the band plays very loudly!

The group has encouraged many deaf people, and people with other disabilities, to follow their dreams. Chevy says, "The only thing deaf people *can't* do is hear."

Dennis McCarthy, "Deaf band 'Beethoven's Nightmare' feels the music," *Los Angeles Daily News* (Oct. 31, 2013). Used with permission.

B Read the article. Choose the correct word(s) in the sentences below.

1. After going deaf, Beethoven **continued / refused** to compose music.
2. The boys knew music was powerful because of something they **read / saw.**
3. Many people didn't **understand / like** the boys' ambition to play music.
4. Hiltermann's parents **wanted / didn't want** him to learn to play at first.
5. The three young men started playing together **before / after** finishing college.

C Answer the questions.

1. Which band inspired the three boys to play music?
2. What did Longo and Chevy use to hear some parts of the music?
3. What did Hiltermann use to make noise in his house?
4. Where did the three men get to know each other?
5. When did Beethoven's Nightmare start playing?

D Do you think it's very difficult for people in your country to achieve their dreams? What new technology and facilities make it easier for them?

SELF-ASSESSMENT

How well can you do these things? Check (✓) the boxes.

I can . . .	Very well	OK	A little
Give information about books, movies, songs, etc. (Ex. 1)	☐	☐	☐
Understand information about countries (Ex. 2)	☐	☐	☐
Describe a situation (Ex. 3)	☐	☐	☐
Ask and answer questions about past events (Ex. 4, 5)	☐	☐	☐
Ask and answer questions about recent activities (Ex. 5)	☐	☐	☐

1 SPEAKING Trivia questions

A List six books, movies, songs, albums, or other popular works. Then write one *who* question for each of the six items.

> *Harry Potter books*
> *Who wrote the Harry Potter books?*

B PAIR WORK Take turns asking your questions. Use the passive with *by* to answer.

A: Who wrote the *Harry Potter* books?
B: I think they were written by J. K. Rowling.

2 LISTENING Did you know?

▶ **A** Listen to a game show about Spain. Write the correct answers.

1. How many languages are officially recognized? _____
2. What day is considered bad luck? _____
3. What is the most valuable soccer team in the world? _____
4. In how many countries is Spanish the official language? _____
5. What fruit is thrown at the world's biggest food fight? _____
6. What is Spain's famous dance called? _____

▶ **B** Listen again. Keep score. How much money does each contestant have?

3 GAME What happened?

GROUP WORK Use the passive to write details about these situations. Then compare with the class. Which group wrote the most sentences?

The lights went out.	It snowed a lot yesterday.	Your roommate cleaned the apartment.
Our class was canceled.	Many roads were blocked.	The dishes were done.

4 ROLE PLAY Do you have an alibi?

A famous painting has been stolen from a local museum. It disappeared last Sunday afternoon between 12:00 P.M. and 4:00 P.M.

Student A: Student B suspects you stole the painting. Make up an alibi. Take notes on what you were doing that day. Then answer Student B's questions.

Student B: You are a police detective. You think Student A stole the painting. Add two questions to the notebook. Then ask Student A the questions.

Change roles and try the role play again.

Where were you last Sunday?

Where did you go for lunch?

Did anyone see you?

What were you wearing that day?

What were you doing between noon and 4:00 P.M.?

Was anyone with you?

_____

_____

5 DISCUSSION Is that so?

A GROUP WORK What interesting things can you find out about your classmates? Ask these questions and others of your own.

Have you been doing anything exciting recently?

Where do you live? How long have you been living there?

Have you met anyone interesting lately?

Who is your best friend? How did you meet? How long have you been friends?

Where were you living ten years ago? Did you like it there? What do you remember about it?

useful expressions

Really?

I didn't know that!

Oh, I see.

I had no idea.

Wow! Tell me more.

B CLASS ACTIVITY Tell the class the most interesting thing you learned.

WHAT'S NEXT?

Look at your Self-assessment again. Do you need to review anything?

13 That's entertainment!

▸ Discuss popular entertainment
▸ Discuss movies and famous Hollywood names

1 SNAPSHOT

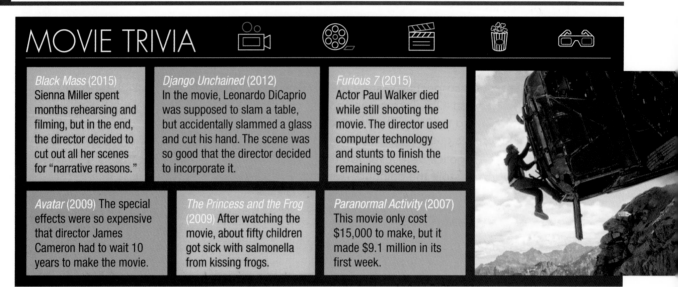

MOVIE TRIVIA

Black Mass (2015) Sienna Miller spent months rehearsing and filming, but in the end, the director decided to cut out all her scenes for "narrative reasons."

Django Unchained (2012) In the movie, Leonardo DiCaprio was supposed to slam a table, but accidentally slammed a glass and cut his hand. The scene was so good that the director decided to incorporate it.

Furious 7 (2015) Actor Paul Walker died while still shooting the movie. The director used computer technology and stunts to finish the remaining scenes.

Avatar (2009) The special effects were so expensive that director James Cameron had to wait 10 years to make the movie.

The Princess and the Frog (2009) After watching the movie, about fifty children got sick with salmonella from kissing frogs.

Paranormal Activity (2007) This movie only cost $15,000 to make, but it made $9.1 million in its first week.

Which of the movie trivia do you find most interesting?

Do you know any other movie trivia?

Which of these movies have you seen? Did you enjoy it? Which would you like to watch?

2 CONVERSATION I think they're boring.

▶ **A** Listen and practice.

Danny: It's so hot out. Do you want to stay in and watch a movie this afternoon?

Gina: Hmm. Maybe. What do you want to see?

Danny: How about an *X-Men* movie? I've heard that the early ones are really interesting.

Gina: For you, maybe. I'm not interested in action movies. Actually, I think they're boring.

Danny: What about that new movie based on one of Stephen King's novels?

Gina: I don't know. I'm always fascinated by his books, but I'm not in the mood for a horror movie.

Danny: Well, what do you want to see?

Gina: How about a *Game of Thrones* marathon? It's my favorite series ever.

Danny: OK, but only if you make us some popcorn.

▶ **B** Listen to the rest of the conversation. What happens next? What do they decide to do?

3 GRAMMAR FOCUS

▶ Participles as adjectives

Present participles	Past participles
That *X-Men* movie sounds **interesting**.	I'm not **interested** in action movies.
Stephen King's books are **fascinating**.	I'm **fascinated** by Stephen King's books.
I think action movies are **boring**.	I'm **bored** by action movies.

GRAMMAR PLUS *see page 144*

A Complete these sentences. Then compare with a partner.

1. John Cho is such an _____ actor. I'm always _____ by his incredible talent. (amaze)
2. Most TV shows are really _____. I often get so _____ watching them that I fall asleep. (bore)
3. I was _____ in watching *The Martian* after I read the book. And I was surprised that the movie is really _____. (interest)
4. I'm _____ to watch *The Avengers*. Everybody has told me it's really _____. (excite)
5. I find animated films very _____. I've been _____ by them since I was a little kid. (amuse / fascinate)
6. It's _____ that horror movies are so popular. I can't understand why people go to the movies to feel _____. (surprise / terrify)

John Cho

B **PAIR WORK** Complete the description below with the correct forms of the words.

> amaze   annoy   confuse   disgust   embarrass   shock

I had a terrible time at the movies last weekend. First, my ticket cost $25. I was really _____ by the price. By mistake, I gave the cashier two $5 bills instead of a twenty and a five. I was a little _____. Then there was trash all over the theater. The mess was _____. The people behind me were talking during the movie, which was _____. The story was hard to follow. I always find thrillers so _____. I liked the special effects, though. They were _____!

4 WORD POWER How do you like it?

A **PAIR WORK** Complete the chart with synonyms from the list.

amusing	dumb	horrible	odd	silly
bizarre	fantastic	hysterical	outstanding	terrible
disgusting	hilarious	incredible	ridiculous	weird

Awful	Wonderful	Stupid	Strange	Funny

B **GROUP WORK** Share your opinions about a movie, an actor, an actress, a TV show, and a book. Use words from part A.

5 LISTENING What did you think?

▶ **A** Listen to people talk about books, movies, and TV programs. Match each conversation to the statement that best describes the people's opinions.

1. ___   **a.** This special offers an amazing look into an exotic country.
2. ___   **b.** The new investigation into these creatures was a waste of time.
3. ___   **c.** The bad acting with this boring idea makes it terrible.
4. ___   **d.** She is excited to read more of this clever mystery series.

▶ **B** Listen again. Write a reason each person gives to support his or her opinion.

1. _____   3. _____
2. _____   4. _____

6 PRONUNCIATION Emphatic stress

▶ **A** Listen and practice. Notice how stress and a higher pitch are used to express strong opinions.

That was terrible!

He was amazing!

That's fascinating!

B **PAIR WORK** Write four statements using these words. Then take turns reading them. Pay attention to emphatic stress.

fantastic   horrible   ridiculous   weird

7 DISCUSSION I give it two thumbs up!

A **PAIR WORK** Take turns asking and answering these questions and others of your own.

What kinds of movies are you interested in? Why?
What kinds of movies do you find boring?
Who are your favorite actors and actresses? Why?
Are there actors or actresses you don't like?
What's the worst movie you've ever seen?
Are there any outstanding movies playing now?
Do you prefer to watch films dubbed or with subtitles? Why?

A: What kinds of movies are you interested in?
B: I like romantic comedies.
A: Really? Why is that?
B: They're entertaining! What about you?
A: I think romantic comedies are kind of dumb. I prefer . . .

B **GROUP WORK** Compare your information. Whose taste in movies is most like yours?

ACTION
COMEDY
ANIMATION
FANTASY
BIOGRAPHY
SCI-FI
THRILLER
HORROR
DRAMA
WAR
DOCUMENTARY

▶ **A** Listen to people talk about some of their Hollywood favorites.
Can you guess the actress, actor, or movie each person is describing?

1. He's a famous American actor who is also a successful director and producer. He won the Oscar for Best Motion Picture in 2013 with *Argo*, which he directed and co-produced.

2. The first movie in the series came out in 1977. It's a science fiction fantasy that has become a blockbuster franchise. The story takes place "a long time ago in a galaxy far, far away."

3. I really like animated movies, and the third one in this series is my favorite. It's about a boy's toys that have a secret life full of adventures when they are alone.

4. She's an actress that is excellent in both dramas and comedies. I loved her in *Mamma Mia!* and *The Devil Wears Prada*. In 2011, she won her third Oscar for her performance in *The Iron Lady*.

B Do you like the people and movies described in part A? What else do you know about them?

9 GRAMMAR FOCUS

▶ **Relative pronouns for people and things**

Use *who* or *that* for people.	**Use *which* or *that* for things.**
He's an actor. He's also a director and producer.	It's a science fiction fantasy. It has become a blockbuster franchise.
He's an actor **who/that** is also a director and producer.	It's a science fiction fantasy **which/that** has become a blockbuster franchise.

GRAMMAR PLUS *see page 144*

Jennifer Hudson

A Combine the sentences using relative pronouns. Then compare with a partner.

1. Jennifer Hudson is a singer. She's acted in several films.
2. *The Phantom of the Opera* is based on a French novel. It was published in 1911.
3. *Spiderman* and *Transformers* are successful franchises. They were adapted from comic books.
4. Michael Keaton is a famous Hollywood actor. He began his career as a cameraman.
5. Dakota Fanning is an actress. She made her first movie when she was only seven years old.
6. Wii Fit is a video game. It helps people to get more exercise.
7. Stephenie Meyer is an American writer. She wrote the *Twilight* series.
8. Many Hollywood stars live in Beverly Hills. It's a small city near Los Angeles, California.

B **PAIR WORK** Complete these sentences. Then compare your information around the class.

1. Adele is a singer and songwriter . . .
2. *Fantastic Four* is a movie franchise . . .
3. *The Voice* is a reality show . . .
4. Scarlett Johansson is an actress . . .

10 INTERCHANGE 13 It was hilarious!

How do you like movies and TV shows? Go to Interchange 13 on page 127.

11 SPEAKING Pilot episode

A PAIR WORK A TV studio is looking for ideas for a new TV show. Brainstorm possible ideas and agree on an idea. Make brief notes.

What kind of TV show is it?
What's it about?
Who are the main characters?
Who is this show for?

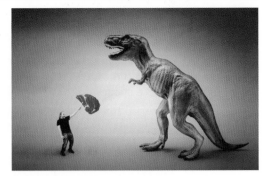

B CLASS ACTIVITY Tell the class about your TV show.

"Our TV show is a comedy. It's about two very lazy friends who discover a time machine and travel to the time of the dinosaurs. Then . . ."

12 LISTENING At the movies

A Listen to two critics, Nicole and Anthony, talk about a new movie. Check (✓) the features of the movie that they discuss. (There are two extra features.)

		Nicole's opinion	Anthony's opinion
☐	acting		
☐	story		
☐	writing		
☐	music		
☐	love story		
☐	special effects		

B Listen again. Write Nicole and Anthony's opinions of each feature.

13 WRITING A movie review

A PAIR WORK Choose a movie you both have seen and discuss it. Then write a review of it.

What was the movie about?
What did you like about it?
What didn't you like about it?
How was the acting?
How would you rate it?

B CLASS ACTIVITY Read your review to the class. Who else has seen the movie?

Do they agree with your review?

MOVIE TALK   LOGIN / REGISTER

We recently streamed *Birdman*, which won the Academy Award for Best Picture in 2015. It's about an actor who made successful movies in Hollywood in the past, and now tries to reinvent his career on Broadway.

BEST PICTURE
BIRDMAN
OR (THE UNEXPECTED VIRTUE OF IGNORANCE)

It stars Michael Keaton and Emma Stone as a father and daughter. We liked the movie because it is both a drama and a comedy. I didn't like . . .

💬 14   ♡ 12

A Scan the article. Which movies are mentioned? When were they released?

THE REAL ART OF ACTING

Natalie Portman

1 **Acting can bring fame, money, and success. But it's not always easy. Good acting is not only about learning lines and dressing up. It's also about convincing the audience that you really are somebody else.** _[a]_ **To achieve this, good actors sometimes put themselves through unpleasant experiences.**

2 Actors often have to lose or gain a lot of weight in order to play a part. In *The Machinist* (2005), Christian Bale plays an extremely thin factory worker who suffers from insomnia. _[b]_ Four months before he began filming, Bale started a crazy diet.

Christian Bale

He only ate an apple and a can of tuna a day and lost 63 pounds. Although he wanted to lose another 20 pounds, the producers persuaded him to stop because they were worried about his health. When filming ended, he had just six months to gain the incredible 100 pounds he needed to play Bruce Wayne in *Batman Begins*. _[c]_

3 Physical training can also be a challenge. Steven Spielberg wanted to show the real horror of war in *Saving Private Ryan* (1998) and he wanted his actors to feel like real soldiers. So he sent a group of them, including Tom Hanks, to a 10-day military boot camp. _[d]_ They ran miles every day, slept outside in the freezing cold, and were given little food. In the end, all of them were physically and mentally exhausted. Natalie Portman also had to make a great physical effort when she got the role of a ballerina in *Black Swan* (2010). Before filming, she spent a whole year training for eight hours a day, six days

a week in order to learn to dance. Once filming began, things didn't get easier either. Portman dislocated a rib while dancing. Nevertheless, she bravely continued filming during the six weeks it took her to recover.

4 Sometimes "becoming" a character can mean saying goodbye to the real world and everybody in it completely. Actor Heath Ledger locked himself in a hotel room for six weeks when he was preparing to play the role of Joker in *The Dark Knight* (2008). He slept only two hours a day and he spent the rest of the time practicing how to walk, talk, and move like his character. _[e]_ It seems he was successful in the end, as audiences and critics loved his work, and he won an Oscar for the part.

B Read the article. Where do these sentences belong? Write a–e.

1. The actors' lives became very hard. ____
2. Not sleeping is making him sick. ____
3. And he didn't speak to anybody at all. ____
4. The character has to be believable. ____
5. So he ate lots of pizza and ice cream. ____

C Find words in the text to match these definitions.

1. The words that actors say in a movie (paragraph 1) _____
2. People who control how a movie is made (paragraph 2) _____
3. A bone in a person's chest (paragraph 3) _____
4. The people who write reviews of movies or books (paragraph 4) _____

D Which of these unpleasant experiences is the worst? Do you think it's necessary for an actor to do this kind of thing for a part?

14 Now I get it!

▸ Discuss the meaning of gestures and body language
▸ Discuss rules and recognize common signs

1 SNAPSHOT

POPULAR EMOJIS

I am not amused.

I'm laughing so hard, I'm crying!

I'm bored.

Great job!

That's amazing!

I'm so embarrassed.

I love it!

That's awful!

Just kidding!

My heart is breaking.

Do you use these emojis? In what situations do you use them?
What other expressions can you use emojis to convey?
What is the weirdest emoji you've ever seen? the funniest? the hardest to understand?

2 WORD POWER Body language

A What is this woman doing in each picture? Match each description with a picture. Then compare with a partner.

1. She's scratching her head. _____
2. She's biting her nails. _____
3. She's rolling her eyes. _____
4. She's tapping her foot. _____
5. She's pulling her hair out. _____
6. She's wrinkling her nose. _____

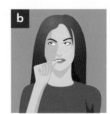

B GROUP WORK Use the pictures in part A and these adjectives to describe how the woman is feeling.

annoyed	confused	embarrassed	frustrated	irritated
bored	disgusted	exhausted	impatient	nervous

"In the first picture, she's tapping her foot. She looks impatient."

3 CONVERSATION It's pretty confusing.

▶ **A** Listen and practice.

Eva: How was dinner with the new Bulgarian student last night? What's her name – Elena?

Brian: Yeah, Elena. It was nice. We always have a good time, but I still don't understand her very well. You see, when we offer her something to eat or drink, she nods her head up and down. But, at the same time she says no.

Eva: It might mean she wants to accept it, but she thinks it's not polite. In some countries, you have to refuse any offer first. Then the host insists, and you accept it.

Brian: I don't know . . . It's pretty confusing.

Eva: It could mean she doesn't want anything, but she thinks it's rude to say no.

Jack: Actually, in some countries, when people move their heads up and down, it means "no."

Brian: Really? Now I get it!

▶ **B** Now listen to Elena talk to her friend. What does she find unusual about the way people in North America communicate?

4 GRAMMAR FOCUS

▶ **Modals and adverbs**

Modals	**Adverbs**
It **might/may** mean she wants to accept it.	**Maybe/Perhaps** it means she wants to accept it.
It **could** mean she doesn't want anything.	It **probably** means she doesn't want anything.
That **must** mean "no."	That **definitely** means "no."

GRAMMAR PLUS *see page 145*

PAIR WORK What do these gestures mean? Take turns making statements about each gesture. Use the meanings in the box or your own ideas.

possible meanings

I don't know.

Be quiet.

Call me.

That sounds crazy!

I can't hear you.

Come here.

A: What do you think the first gesture means?

B: It probably means . . . , OR It might mean . . .

5 PRONUNCIATION Pitch

▶ **A** Listen and practice. Notice how pitch is used to express certainty or doubt.

	Certain	**Uncertain**
A: Do you think her gesture means "no"?	**B:** Definitely.	**B:** Probably.
A: Do you understand what her gesture means?	**B:** Absolutely.	**B:** Maybe.

B PAIR WORK Take turns asking yes/no questions. Respond by using *absolutely*, *definitely*, *maybe*, *probably*, and your own information. Pay attention to pitch.

6 SPEAKING What's the matter with me?

A GROUP WORK Imagine you have one of these problems. What could explain it?

I'm always late for class.

I'm always exhausted at the end of the day.

I'm often irritated with everybody at the office.

I'm often bored.

I'm always broke.

I often argue with my friends.

A: I'm always exhausted at the end of the day.
B: It might mean you are not getting enough sleep.
C: It could mean you are working too hard.
D: That definitely means . . .

B CLASS ACTIVITY Who came up with the most interesting explanation in your group? the most unexpected?

7 INTERCHANGE 14 Casual observers

Interpret people's body language. Go to Interchange 14 on page 128.

8 PERSPECTIVES Rules and regulations

A What do you think these signs mean? Listen and match each sign with the correct meaning.

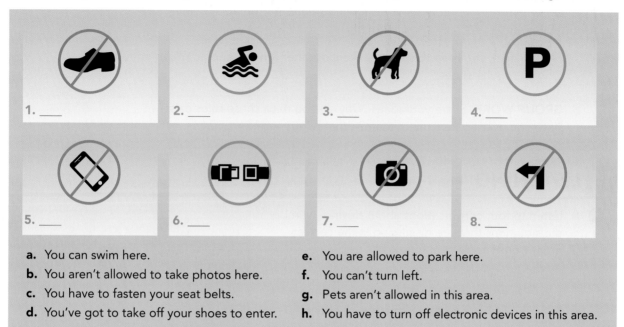

1. ____   2. ____   3. ____   4. ____

5. ____   6. ____   7. ____   8. ____

a. You can swim here.
b. You aren't allowed to take photos here.
c. You have to fasten your seat belts.
d. You've got to take off your shoes to enter.

e. You are allowed to park here.
f. You can't turn left.
g. Pets aren't allowed in this area.
h. You have to turn off electronic devices in this area.

B PAIR WORK Where might you see the signs in part A? Give two suggestions for each one.

"You might see this one by a lake . . ."

9 GRAMMAR FOCUS

Permission, obligation, and prohibition

Permission	Obligation	Prohibition
You **can** swim here.	You **have to** fasten your seat belt.	You **can't** turn left.
You**'re allowed to** park here.	You**'ve got to** take off your shoes.	Pets **aren't allowed** in this area.

GRAMMAR PLUS *see page 145*

A PAIR WORK Use the language in the grammar box to talk about these signs.

A: This first sign means you've got to use the stairs in case of a fire.
B: Yes, I think you're right. And the second one means you aren't allowed to . . .

B CLASS ACTIVITY What are some of the rules in your office or school?

A: In my office, we can't eat at our desks.
B: We can't either, but we're allowed to have water.
C: We're allowed to eat at our desks, but we have to clean up afterward.

10 DISCUSSION Play by the rules.

A PAIR WORK How many rules can you think of for each of these places?

at the gym   at a public swimming pool   on an airplane
in a museum   in a movie theater   at work

"At the gym, you have to wear sneakers or other athletic shoes. You're not allowed to wear regular shoes."

B GROUP WORK Share your ideas. Why do you think these rules exist? Have you ever broken any of them? What happened?

11 LISTENING Road signs

▶ **A** Listen to four conversations about driving. Number the situations they are discussing in the correct order from 1 to 4.

_____ Cars can't be in the bus and taxi lane.
_____ Drivers must drive within the speed limit.
_____ Drivers have to turn on car headlights on mountain roads.
_____ Cars are allowed to park in this area after 6:00 P.M.

▶ **B** Listen again. How did they find out about the traffic situation? Write what happened.

1. _____
2. _____
3. _____
4. _____

C PAIR WORK How do you move around your city? Give two examples of traffic laws you must obey.

12 WRITING Golden rules

A GROUP WORK Discuss the rules that currently exist at your school. How many can you think of? Are they all good rules?

B GROUP WORK Think of four new rules that you feel would be a good idea. Work together to write brief explanations of why each is necessary.

1. You aren't allowed to use your first language. If you need to use it, you need to ask your teacher for permission.
2. You have to pay a small fine if you hand in your homework late.
3. You can be late, but you have to come in quietly so you don't disturb the lesson.

C CLASS ACTIVITY Share your lists. Vote on the best new rules.

A Skim the article. Match the pictures 1, 2, and 3 to the paragraphs.

— U N D E R S T A N D I N G   I D I O M S —

Idioms can be a problem for language learners. They often seem to make absolutely no sense at all. For example, imagine your English friend Sam tells you his math exam was "a piece of cake." Do you imagine him at school, sitting in front of a sweet dessert with nothing but a pen to eat it with? In fact, he's saying that the exam was really easy. It's important to learn useful English idioms and knowing their origins helps us to remember them. Here are stories of three English idioms.

____ **A** If you ask a friend to hang out, you might hear, "Sorry, I can't tonight. I'm feeling a little under the weather." It may sound like rain is coming, but really, it means that your friend feels sick. This expression came from sailors, who often got seasick when bad weather tossed the ship from side to side. The sailors went down to the bottom part of the ship, away from the storm and where the ship's rocking was gentler.

____ **B** If you have a difficult roommate, you might say, "My roommate has loud parties every night, but last night was the last straw. They played music till 5 A.M.! I'm moving out." A "last straw" is a final problem that makes someone take action. This expression is a short form of the phrase "the straw that broke the camel's back." The idea is that even though a single piece of straw is very light, many pieces added together will be too heavy for the camel to carry.

____ **C** Have you ever asked someone if they know something, and they reply, "That rings a bell"? They're not hearing music! They mean that what you're saying sounds familiar, and they think they've heard it before. This idiom comes from the fact that bells are used to remind people of many things. Traditionally, bells would toll for an important event, like a wedding. School bells tell you that class is starting, and even the alarm chime on your phone reminds you that it's time to get up.

B Read the article and correct the false statements below.

1. You can guess the meaning of an idiom if you understand each word.

_____

2. In the past, people knew about important events when they heard shouting.

_____

3. A camel falls down if it has to carry too much water.

_____

4. Sailors used to feel sicker when they went to the bottom of the ship.

_____

C Complete the sentences with the correct form of one of the idioms.

1. Julie has a bad cold at the moment, and she's _____.

2. I don't remember his face, but his name _____.

3. When the neighbors' noisy kids broke my window with their ball, it _____.

D What idioms are commonly used in your country? Where do you think they come from?

Units 13–14 Progress check

SELF-ASSESSMENT

How well can you do these things? Check (✓) the boxes.

I can . . .	Very well	OK	A little
Ask about and express opinions and emotions (Ex. 1, 4, 5)	☐	☐	☐
Discuss movies (Ex. 2)	☐	☐	☐
Understand descriptions of rules and laws (Ex. 3)	☐	☐	☐
Speculate about things when I'm not sure and recognize emotions (Ex. 4)	☐	☐	☐
Describe rules and laws: permission, obligation, and prohibition (Ex. 5)	☐	☐	☐

1 SURVEY   Personal preferences

A Complete the first column of the survey with your opinions.

	Me	My classmate
A fascinating book		
A confusing movie		
A boring TV show		
A shocking news story		
An interesting celebrity		
A singer you are amazed by		
A song you are annoyed by		

B CLASS ACTIVITY Go around the class and find someone who has
the same opinions. Write a classmate's name only once.

"I thought *I am Malala* was a fascinating book. What about you?"

2 ROLE PLAY   Movie night

Student A: Invite Student B to a movie. Suggest two movie options.
Then answer your partner's questions.
Start like this: *Do you want to see a movie?*

Student B: Student A invites you to a movie.
Find out more about the movie.
Then accept or refuse the invitation.

Change roles and try the role play again.

3 LISTENING Unusual laws around the world

▶ **A** Listen to two people discuss an article about laws in different places. Match the topic to the place. (There are two extra topics.)

a. smiling	b. chewing gum	c. stealing
d. hospitals	e. pigeons	f. carrying money

1. Singapore ____   **2.** Kenya ____   **3.** San Francisco ____   **4.** Milan ____

▶ **B** Listen again. Complete the sentences to describe each law.

1. In Singapore, you _____.

2. In Kenya, you _____.

3. In San Francisco, you _____.

4. In Milan, you _____.

C **PAIR WORK** Which law seems the strangest to you? the most logical? Why?

4 GAME Miming

A Think of two emotions or ideas you can communicate with gestures. Write them on separate cards.

B **GROUP WORK** Shuffle your cards together. Then take turns picking cards and acting out the meanings with gestures. The student who guesses correctly goes next.

A: That probably means you're disgusted.

B: No.

C: It could mean you're surprised.

B: You're getting closer . . .

I'm confused. I don't understand what you really want.

5 DISCUSSION What's the law?

GROUP WORK Read these laws from the United States. What do you think about them? Are they the same or different in your country?

• You aren't allowed to keep certain wild animals as pets.

• You're allowed to vote when you turn 18.

• In some states, you can get married when you're 16.

• You have to wear a seat belt in the back seat of a car in most states.

• Young men don't have to serve in the military.

• In some states, you can't drive faster than 65 miles per hour (about 100 kph).

• In most states, children have to attend school until they are 16 or 18.

A: In the U.S.A., you aren't allowed to keep certain wild animals as pets.

B: It's the same for us. You've got to have a special permit to keep a wild animal.

C: I've heard that in some countries, you can keep lions and tigers as pets.

WHAT'S NEXT?

Look at your Self-assessment again. Do you need to review anything?

15 I wouldn't have done that.

▶ Discuss imaginary situations
▶ Discuss difficult situations

1 SNAPSHOT

NEWS 4 YOU

| NEW TODAY | MOST POPULAR | TRENDING | LOGIN | SIGN UP |

FLORIDA MOM "CAUGHT" BEING HONEST

Nancy Bloom was caught on the security camera entering a convenience store while the owner was out to lunch. The door was unlocked, so Nancy walked in with her son, picked up some ice cream, and left the money on the counter.

MOST SHARED THIS WEEK

HONESTY IS ITS OWN REWARD

After driving for 20 miles to return a wallet lost in a park, Kate Moore gets only a half-hearted, "Oh. Thanks."

HOMELESS MAN FINDS $40,000 AND TURNS IT IN

When Tom Heart found a backpack full of cash, he didn't think twice. He took it straight to the police. After reading Tom's story, a stranger started a fundraising campaign for Tom that has already raised over $60,000.

Have you heard any stories like these recently?
Have you ever found anything valuable? What did you do?
Do you think that people who return lost things should get a reward?

2 CONVERSATION What would you do?

▶ **A** Listen and practice.

Joon: Look at this. A homeless guy found a backpack with $40,000 inside!

Mia: And what did he do?

Joon: He took it to the police. He gave it all back, every single penny.

Mia: You're kidding! If I found $40,000, I wouldn't return it. I'd keep it.

Joon: Really? What would you do with it?

Mia: Well, I'd spend it. I could buy a new car or take a nice long vacation.

Joon: The real owner might find out about it, though, and then you could go to jail.

Mia: Hmm. You've got a point there.

▶ **B** Listen to the rest of the conversation. What would Joon do if he found $40,000?

3 GRAMMAR FOCUS

▶ **Unreal conditional sentences with *if* clauses**

Imaginary situation (simple past)	Possible consequence (*would*, *could*, or *might* + verb)
If I **found** $40,000,	**I would keep** it.
	I wouldn't return it.
	I could buy a new car.
	I might go to the police.

What **would** you **do if** you **found** $40,000?

GRAMMAR PLUS see page 146

A Complete these conversations. Then compare with a partner.

1. **A:** What _____ you _____ (do) if you lost your sister's favorite sweater?
   B: Of course I _____ (buy) her a new one.

2. **A:** If you _____ (have) three months to travel, where _____ you _____ (go)?
   B: Oh, that's easy! I _____ (fly) to Europe. I've always wanted to go there.

3. **A:** If your doctor _____ (tell) you to get more exercise, which activity _____ you _____ (choose)?
   B: I'm not sure, but I think I _____ (go) jogging two or three times a week.

4. **A:** _____ you _____ (break) into your house if you _____ (lock) yourself out?
   B: No way! If I _____ (not have) another key, I _____ (ask) a neighbor for help.

5. **A:** If your friend _____ (want) to marry someone you didn't like, _____ you _____ (say) something?
   B: No, I _____ (not say) anything. I _____ (mind) my own business.

6. **A:** What _____ you _____ (do) if you _____ (see) your favorite movie star on the street?
   B: I _____ (not be) shy! I _____ (ask) to take a photo with them.

B **PAIR WORK** Take turns asking the questions in part A. Answer with your own information.

4 LISTENING Tough situations

▶ **A** Listen to three people talk about predicaments. Check which predicament they are talking about.

1. ☐ Chris has relationship problems.   ☐ Chris is addicted to the Internet.
2. ☐ Kari spent all her money in Europe.   ☐ Kari lost all her money in Europe.
3. ☐ Zoey saw her classmates cheating.   ☐ Zoey doesn't understand her math class.

▶ **B** Listen again. Write the two suggestions given for each predicament.

1. **a.** _____   **b.** _____
2. **a.** _____   **b.** _____
3. **a.** _____   **b.** _____

C **GROUP WORK** Which suggestions do you agree with? Why?

5 INTERCHANGE 15 Tough choices

What would you do in some difficult situations? Go to Interchange 15 on page 130.

6 WORD POWER Opposites

A Find nine pairs of opposites in this list. Complete the chart. Then compare with a partner.

accept	borrow	dislike	find	lose	remember
admit	deny	divorce	forget	marry	save
agree	disagree	enjoy	lend	refuse	spend

accept	≠	refuse		≠			≠
	≠			≠			≠
	≠			≠			≠

B **PAIR WORK** Choose four pairs of opposites. Write sentences using each pair.

> I can't remember my dreams. As soon as I wake up, I forget them.

7 PERSPECTIVES That was a big mistake.

▶ **A** Listen to people talk about recent predicaments. Then check (✓) the best suggestion for each one.

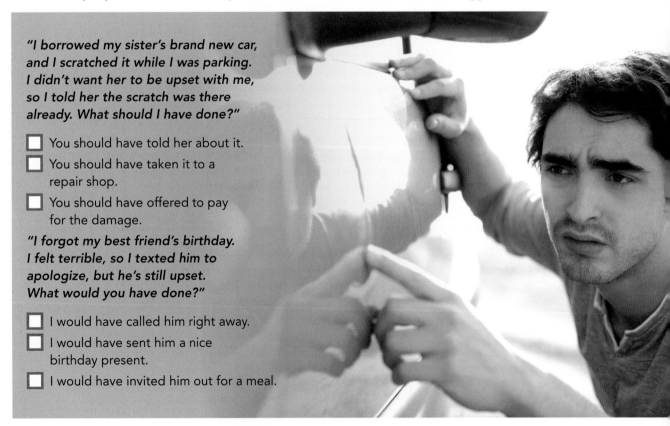

"I borrowed my sister's brand new car, and I scratched it while I was parking. I didn't want her to be upset with me, so I told her the scratch was there already. What should I have done?"

☐ You should have told her about it.
☐ You should have taken it to a repair shop.
☐ You should have offered to pay for the damage.

"I forgot my best friend's birthday. I felt terrible, so I texted him to apologize, but he's still upset. What would you have done?"

☐ I would have called him right away.
☐ I would have sent him a nice birthday present.
☐ I would have invited him out for a meal.

B **PAIR WORK** Compare with a partner. Do you agree with each other?

8 GRAMMAR FOCUS

> **Past modals** ·
>
> Use *would have* or *should have* + past participle to give opinions or suggestions about actions in the past.
>
> | What **should** I **have done**? | You **should have told** her about it. |
> | | You **shouldn't have lied** to your sister. |
> | What **would** you **have done**? | I **would have called** him. |
> | | I **wouldn't have texted** him. |
>
> **GRAMMAR PLUS** *see page 146*

A Complete these conversations. Then practice with a partner.

1. **A:** I was in a meeting at work when my girlfriend texted me saying she needed to see me right away. What should I have _____ (do)?
   B: You should have _____ (send) her a message and _____ (tell) her you'd call back later.

2. **A:** The cashier gave me too much change. What should I have _____ (do)?
   B: You should have _____ (say) something. You shouldn't have _____ (take) the money.

3. **A:** I ignored an email from someone I don't like. What would you have _____ (do)?
   B: I would have _____ (reply) to the person. It just takes a minute!

4. **A:** We left all our trash at the campsite. What would you have _____ (do)?
   B: I would have _____ (take) it with me and _____ (throw) it away later.

B Read the situations below. What would have been the best thing to do? Choose suggestions. Then compare with a partner.

Situations

1. The teacher borrowed my favorite book and spilled coffee all over it. _____
2. I saw a classmate cheating on an exam, so I wrote her an email about it. _____
3. A friend of mine always has messy hair, so I gave him a comb for his birthday. _____
4. I hit someone's car when I was leaving a parking lot. Luckily, no one saw me. _____
5. My aunt gave me a wool sweater. I can't wear wool, so I gave it back. _____

Suggestions

a. You should have spoken to him about it.
b. I would have spoken to the teacher about it.
c. I would have waited for the owner to return.
d. I wouldn't have said anything.
e. You should have warned her not to do it again.
f. You should have left a note for the owner.
g. I would have told her that I prefer something else.
h. You should have exchanged it for something else.

C **GROUP WORK** Make another suggestion for each situation in part B.

9 PRONUNCIATION Reduction of *have*

A Listen and practice. Notice how **have** is reduced in these sentences.

/əv/
What would you have done?

/əv/
I would have told the truth.

B **PAIR WORK** Practice the conversations in Exercise 8, part A, again. Use the reduced form of **have**.

10 LISTENING Problem solved!

▶ **A** Listen to an advice podcast. Complete the chart.

	Problem	What the person did
Ronnie:		
Becca:		

▶ **B** Listen again. According to Dr. Jones, what should each person have done?

Ronnie: _____

Becca: _____

C **PAIR WORK** What would you have done in each situation?

11 SPEAKING An awful trip

A **PAIR WORK** Imagine a friend has been on a really awful trip and everything went wrong. What should your friend have done? What shouldn't he or she have done?

Your friend spent hours in the sun and got a sunburn.
Your friend drank tap water and got sick.
Your friend stayed at a very bad hotel.
Your friend's wallet was stolen.
Your friend overslept and missed the flight back.

A: She shouldn't have spent so many hours in the sun.
B: She should have used sunscreen.

B **GROUP WORK** Have you ever had any bad experiences on a trip? What happened?

12 WRITING Advice needed

Write a post to a community blog about a real or imaginary problem.
Put your drafts on the wall and choose one to write a reply to.

● ● ● ‹ ›   🔍 🏠

WHAT WENT WRONG?

submitted by dmartin 10 hours ago

I lent my girlfriend $10,000 to help her pay for her college tuition. That was about a year ago, and at the time, she said she would pay me back as soon as she found a job. She never even looked for a job. Last week, I asked her for my money back, and she accused me of being selfish, unsympathetic, and insensitive. She broke up with me, and now she won't even talk to me anymore. What did I do wrong? What should I have done? What should I do now? Does anyone have any suggestions?

248 comments

A Skim the three posts. What do Jack, Maya, and Andrés ask for advice about?

TOPTIPS.COM

HOME   NEW   ABOUT   COMMUNITY   👤 SIGN IN

1 JACK – LONDON   ♡ 12

I am overweight, and I'd really like to slim down. I've tried all kinds of diets, but none of them seem to work. And there's so much advice on the Internet – I don't know what to believe any more. What would you recommend?

I had the same problem until I tried a high protein/no carbohydrate diet. It was very strict – in the first couple of weeks you have to eat less than 40 grams of carbohydrates a day, so no bread, pasta, or potatoes! But I lost nine pounds in just 13 days, so for me it was worth it. I had a lot of meat and eggs and some butter, too, which was great! I'd give it a shot if I were you. (Sarah, Edinburgh)

2 MAYA – SAN FRANCISCO   ♡ 22

I'm traveling to Rio de Janeiro next month, and I'd like to see as much of the city as possible. The problem is that I'm only going to be there for a couple of days, and I'm not sure how to fit everything in. Should I book an organized tour?

I was in Rio a couple of months ago. I travel a lot and like to be independent, so I chose to find my own way around the city. What a mistake! Rio's so big that I kept getting lost! And in the end, I didn't get to see the beach of Ipanema or the cathedral. It would have been nice to have somebody to talk to also. I really should have gone on a guided tour. (Dag, Oslo)

3 ANDRÉS – BOGOTÁ   ♡ 11

I've just finished my degree, and I'm on the fence about what to do next. Here in Bogotá, there aren't many job possibilities right now. Should I go back to college to get a Master's? Or go stay with my cousin in New York and try to get a job there? (My English is not very good, by the way – a friend wrote this!)

Stay where you are! I moved to the United States from Poland and got a job as a server, but it's long hours and not much money. I haven't really made many friends, and I miss home. I should have stayed there and continued with my studies. (Marta, Krakow)

B Read the posts. Who would say these sentences? Write names from the posts.

1. Should I go abroad or stay where I am? _____

2. It worked for me, so why don't you try it? _____

3. I would have been happier if I hadn't moved. _____

4. How can I choose the right eating plan? _____

5. If I went there again, I'd definitely join a group. _____

6. I don't have much time, so I need to be organized. _____

C Find words or expressions in the posts to match these definitions.

1. Be an important or useful thing to do (post 1) _____

2. Find enough time for something (post 2) _____

3. To be unable to make a decision (post 3) _____

D Do you agree with the advice given above? What advice would you give?

16 Making excuses

▶ Give reasons and explanations
▶ Discuss statements other people made

1 SNAPSHOT

Good Excuses, Poor Excuses

Not doing homework
- I was sure the assignment was due tomorrow.
- I emailed it to you, but it bounced back.

Arriving late to class
- My father didn't wake me up.
- My bike tire was flat because a dog bit it.

Missing work
- My cat was sick, and I had to take care of her.
- It was my birthday, and I always donate blood on that day.

Arriving late to work
- I worked on the new project until four in the morning, and then I overslept.
- My wife thinks it's funny to hide my car keys in the morning.

Arriving late for a date
- I was taking a telephone survey and lost track of the time.
- A horse running on the highway was holding up traffic.

Which are good excuses? Which are poor ones?
What excuse do you usually use for these situations?
What excuses can you make for missing a date or party?

2 PERSPECTIVES At your request

A Who do you think made these requests? Listen and match.

1. She said to arrive on time for the meeting. ____
2. She asked me to pick up some food on the way home. ____
3. He said not to miss practice again. ____
4. She told me to hand in my homework before Friday. ____
5. She said to drink at least six glasses of water a day. ____
6. He asked me not to tell Mom about his new girlfriend. ____
7. He told me not to leave my bike in the apartment hallway. ____

a. my teacher
b. my boss
c. my brother
d. my doctor
e. my neighbor
f. my roommate
g. my coach

B **PAIR WORK** Can you think of another request each person might make?

A: Our teacher sometimes says, "Open your books."
B: A teacher could also say, "Repeat after me."

3 GRAMMAR FOCUS

▶ Reported speech: requests

Original request	Reported request
Arrive on time for the meeting.	She **said to arrive** on time for the meeting.
	She **told me to arrive** on time for the meeting.
Don't leave your bike in the apartment hallway.	He **said not to leave** my bike in the hallway.
	He **told me not to leave** my bike in the hallway.
Can you pick up some food on the way home?	She **asked me to pick up** some food.

GRAMMAR PLUS see page 147

A Victor is organizing a surprise birthday party for his teacher. Look at what he told his classmates. Write each request using *say*, *tell*, or *ask*. Then compare with a partner.

1. Meet at my apartment at 7:30. <u>He told them to meet at his apartment at 7:30.</u>
2. Don't arrive late. _____
3. Can you bring some ice cream? _____
4. Can you help me make the sandwiches? _____
5. Can you bring a small gift for her? _____
6. Don't spend more than $10 on the gift. _____
7. Keep the party a secret. _____
8. Don't say anything to the other teachers. _____

B **GROUP WORK** Imagine you're planning a class party. Write four requests. Then take turns reading your requests and changing them into reported requests.

Edu: Bring something to eat to the party!
Eva: Edu told us to bring something to eat.

Aki: Can you help me clean up after the party?
Jim: Aki asked us to help her clean up.

4 SPEAKING That's asking too much!

A Think of requests that people have made recently. Write two things people asked you to do and two things people asked you *not* to do.

Person	Request
My boss	shave off my beard

B **GROUP WORK** Talk about the requests that each of you listed in part A. Did you do what people requested? Did you give an excuse? What was it?

5 WORD POWER Verb-noun collocations

A Find three more nouns that are usually paired with each verb. The same noun can be paired with more than one verb. Then compare with a partner.

an apology	an invitation	a request
a complaint	a joke	a solution
an excuse	a lie	a story
an explanation	an offer	a suggestion
an idea	a reason	the truth

make	_a request_	_____	_____	_____
give	_an excuse_	_____	_____	_____
tell	_a joke_	_____	_____	_____
accept	_an apology_	_____	_____	_____
refuse	_an invitation_	_____	_____	_____

B **PAIR WORK** How do you deal with the things in part A? Tell a partner.

A: What do you do when a close friend makes a difficult request?

B: I give a good explanation, and I offer to help in another way. What about you?

6 CONVERSATION Are you doing anything on Sunday?

▶ **A** Listen and practice.

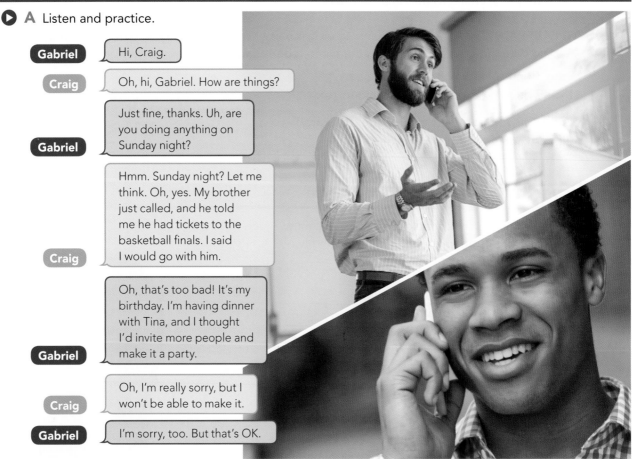

Gabriel Hi, Craig.

Craig Oh, hi, Gabriel. How are things?

Gabriel Just fine, thanks. Uh, are you doing anything on Sunday night?

Craig Hmm. Sunday night? Let me think. Oh, yes. My brother just called, and he told me he had tickets to the basketball finals. I said I would go with him.

Gabriel Oh, that's too bad! It's my birthday. I'm having dinner with Tina, and I thought I'd invite more people and make it a party.

Craig Oh, I'm really sorry, but I won't be able to make it.

Gabriel I'm sorry, too. But that's OK.

B **PAIR WORK** Act out the conversation in part A. Make up your own excuse for not accepting Gabriel's invitation.

7 LISTENING Making excuses

▶ **A** Listen to Gabriel invite his friends to his birthday party on Saturday. What excuses do they give for not going? Write them below.

1. Grant: _____
2. Sayo: _____
3. Diego: _____
4. Carrie: _____

▶ **B** Listen. What happens on the night of Gabriel's birthday?

C **PAIR WORK** What was the last party you went to? Describe it to your partner.

8 GRAMMAR FOCUS

▶ **Reported speech: statements**

Direct statements	Reported statements
I'm **not feeling** well.	She **said** (that) she **wasn't feeling** well.
I **have** houseguests for the weekend.	she **had** houseguests for the weekend.
I **made** a tennis date with Kim.	she **had made** a tennis date with Kim.
I **have planned** an exciting trip.	she **had planned** an exciting trip.
We **can't come** tomorrow.	They **told me** (that) they **couldn't come** tomorrow.
We **will be** out of town.	they **would be** out of town.
We **may go** out with friends.	they **might go** out with friends.

GRAMMAR PLUS *see page 147*

A Isabella is having a party at her house on Saturday. Look at these excuses. Change them into reported speech. Then compare with a partner.

1. Mason: "I already have plans for Saturday."
2. Olivia: "My in-laws are coming over for dinner that night."
3. Ben and Ava: "We've been invited to a graduation party on Saturday."
4. Felipe: "I promised to help my sister with her homework."
5. Tae-yun: "I can't come because I broke my leg."
6. Osvaldo: "I'll be moving this weekend."
7. Lisa and Henry: "We have to pick someone up at the airport that evening."
8. Omar: "I may have to work the night shift on Saturday."

> *Mason said he already had plans for Saturday.* OR
>
> *Mason told her he already had plans for Saturday.*

B **GROUP WORK** Imagine you don't want to go to Isabella's party. Take turns making excuses and changing them into reported speech.

A: I'm sorry, I can't go. I'm going camping this weekend.
B: Lucky guy! He said he was going camping this weekend.

9 PRONUNCIATION Reduction of *had* and *would*

▶ **A** Listen and practice. Notice how *had* and *would* are reduced in the following sentences.

She said she**'d made** the bed. (She said she **had made** the bed.)
She said she**'d make** the bed. (She said she **would make** the bed.)

▶ **B** Listen to four sentences. Check (✓) the reduced form that you hear.

1. ☐ had **2.** ☐ had **3.** ☐ had **4.** ☐ had
☐ would ☐ would ☐ would ☐ would

10 WRITING About my classmates

A Interview your classmates and take notes. Use your notes to write a report describing what people told you. Use reported speech.

	Name	Response
What did you do last night?		
What movie have you seen recently?		
Where are you going after class?		
What are your plans for the weekend?		
What will you do on your next birthday?		

B GROUP WORK Read your report, but don't give names. Others guess the person.

"Someone said that he'd go to Paris on his next vacation."

11 SPEAKING You can make it.

A GROUP WORK What are some things you would like to do in the future? Think of three intentions.

A: I'm going to take an English course abroad.
B: That sounds fun. Have you decided where?

B CLASS ACTIVITY Report the best intentions you heard. Then give suggestions.

B: Noriko said she was going to take an English course abroad, but she hadn't decided where.
C: She could go to Australia. My brother attended a very good school there. He told me he studied incredibly hard!

12 INTERCHANGE 16 Just a bunch of excuses

Make some plans. Student A, go to Interchange 16A on page 129;
Student B, go to Interchange 16B on page 131.

A Scan the article. What are three common reasons for missing work?

A GOOD EXCUSE FOR A
DAY OFF WORK

1 On average, U.S. employees take 4.9 sick days per year. Usually this does not cause any particular problems. But when employees take sick leave without a good reason, it can quickly become an issue. In fact, in one survey, 18 percent of employers said that they had fired an employee for taking days off without a good reason. The key is to understand what reasons are acceptable and what reasons are not. Generally, most excuses for sick days fall into one of three categories.

2 The most common reasons for not going to work are health-related. It would probably be OK to tell your boss that you ate something bad last night and that you have a stomachache. Of course you might not want to share the details of a health issue with your boss – after all, you do have the right to privacy. If you don't want to be too specific, you can just tell your boss that you have a small medical issue and need to take the day off.

3 Household accidents are the second category of reasons for not going in to work. You might call your boss to say you slipped in the shower and hurt your knee. This is a common accident and one that your boss will sympathize with. However, if you are going to be out of work for several days due to an injury, it's important to make arrangements with your employer. See if you can work from home, or at least make sure there is someone to cover your work.

4 The third type of sick day use isn't really about illness, but it's about something else you can't control: transportation problems. The car might not start, there may be a terrible traffic jam, or there could be delays on the subway. Some employers may be sympathetic to absences due to transportation problems, but others may not. It's important to know your boss and to understand whether he or she will accept an excuse like this.

5 Regardless of the reason for the sick day, there are a few things you can do to make missing work more acceptable to your employer. Try to keep sick days to a minimum. When you do need to take a sick day, give your employer as much advance notice as possible. Finally, never take a sick day if there isn't anything wrong with you – the only good excuses are the ones that are true.

B Read the article. Then correct four mistakes in the summary of the article.

U.S. workers take just under a month in sick days a year. The least frequently used excuses are for health reasons. When employees take a sick day, it's important to explain the reason to their colleagues. It's OK to take a sick day, even if you feel fine, as long as you give an excuse.

C Find words in the text to match these definitions.

1. told someone to leave his or her job (paragraph 1) _____
2. an explanation given for something (paragraph 1) _____
3. someone's right to keep information about his or her personal life secret (paragraph 2) _____
4. understand or care about someone's problems (paragraph 3) _____
5. a warning that something is about to happen (paragraph 5) _____

D What other excuses do people make for not going to work or class? What's the silliest excuse you have ever heard?

Units 15–16 Progress check

SELF-ASSESSMENT

How well can you do these things? Check (✓) the boxes.

I can . . .	Very well	OK	A little
Discuss imaginary events (Ex. 1)	☐	☐	☐
Ask for and give advice and suggestions about past events (Ex. 2)	☐	☐	☐
Understand and report requests (Ex. 3)	☐	☐	☐
Discuss statements other people made (Ex. 4)	☐	☐	☐

1 DISCUSSION Interesting situations

A What would you do in these situations? Complete the statements.

If I forgot to do my homework, _____ .
If I found a valuable piece of jewelry in the park, _____ .
If a friend gave me a present I didn't like, _____ .
If I wasn't invited to a party I wanted to attend, _____ .
If someone took my clothes while I was swimming, _____ .

B **GROUP WORK** Compare your responses. For each situation, choose one to tell the class.

A: What would you do if you forgot to do your homework?
B: I'd probably tell the teacher the truth. I'd ask her to let me hand it in next class.

2 SPEAKING Predicaments

A Make up two situations like the one below. Think about experiences you have had or heard about at work, home, or school.

"An old friend from high school visited me recently. We had a great time at first, but he became annoying. He made a big mess, and he left his things all over the place. After two weeks, I told him he had to leave because my sister was coming for the weekend."

B **PAIR WORK** Take turns sharing your situations. Ask for advice and suggestions.

A: What would you have done?
B: Well, I would have told him to pick up his clothes, and I would have asked him to clean up his mess.

3 LISTENING A small request

A Listen to the conversations. Check (✓) the person who is making the request.

1. ☐ child   2. ☐ neighbor   3. ☐ child   4. ☐ teacher   5. ☐ boss   6. ☐ neighbor
   ☐ parent   ☐ teacher   ☐ doctor   ☐ classmate   ☐ neighbor   ☐ teacher

B Listen again. Complete the requests.

1. Please _____ .   4. Can _____ ?
2. Can _____ ?   5. Please _____ .
3. Don't _____ .   6. Can _____ ?

C PAIR WORK Work with a partner. Imagine these requests were for you. Take turns reporting the requests to your partner.

"My dad told me to pick up my things."

4 GAME Who is lying?

A Think of situations when you expressed anger, gave an excuse, or made a complaint. Write a brief statement about each situation.

> I once complained about the bathroom in a hotel.

B CLASS ACTIVITY Play a game. Choose three students to be contestants.

Step 1: The contestants compare their statements and choose one. This statement should be true about only one student. The other two students should pretend they had the experience.

Step 2: The contestants stand in front of the class. Each contestant reads the same statement. The rest of the class must ask questions to find out who isn't telling the truth.

Contestant A, what hotel were you in?

Contestant B, what was wrong with the bathroom?

Contestant C, what did the manager do?

Step 3: Who isn't telling the truth? What did he or she say to make you think that?
"I don't think Contestant B is telling the truth. He said the bathroom was too small!"

WHAT'S NEXT?

Look at your Self-assessment again. Do you need to review anything?

This page is intentionally left blank

Interchange activities

A Read the questions on the cards. Check (✓) the box for your opinion.

1. If teens work part-time, they won't do well in school.
- ☐ I agree.
- ☐ I don't agree.
- ☐ It depends.

2. If kids play violent video games, they will become violent themselves.
- ☐ I agree.
- ☐ I don't agree.
- ☐ It depends.

3. If people decrease their screen time, they'll talk more with their families.
- ☐ I agree.
- ☐ I don't agree.
- ☐ It depends.

4. If a woman gets married very early, she won't invest time in her career.
- ☐ I agree.
- ☐ I don't agree.
- ☐ It depends.

5. If a woman works outside the home, her children won't be happy.
- ☐ I agree.
- ☐ I don't agree.
- ☐ It depends.

6. If a child has brothers and sisters, he or she won't ever feel lonely.
- ☐ I agree.
- ☐ I don't agree.
- ☐ It depends.

7. If you have too many online friends, you'll have fewer "real" friends.
- ☐ I agree.
- ☐ I don't agree.
- ☐ It depends.

8. If there is a heavy fine for littering, our streets will be much cleaner.
- ☐ I agree.
- ☐ I don't agree.
- ☐ It depends.

9. If people work only two days a week, their lives will improve.
- ☐ I agree.
- ☐ I don't agree.
- ☐ It depends.

10. If teens have a lot of freedom, they will get in trouble more often.
- ☐ I agree.
- ☐ I don't agree.
- ☐ It depends.

B **GROUP WORK** Compare your opinions. Be prepared to give reasons for your opinions.

A: I think if teens work part-time, they won't do well in school.
B: I don't really agree.
C: Why not?
B: If they work part-time, they'll become more responsible. That's a positive consequence.

A **PAIR WORK** Look at the following job description. Write an ad for your ideal job.

JOB FINDER   About   Careers   Education   Job search

Activities Director

Requirements:
Experience working with tourists
A "people person"
Outgoing and creative personality

Responsibilities:
Organize all leisure activities on a popular cruise ship, including planning daily tours, special onboard activities, and nightly entertainment

B **PAIR WORK** Take turns interviewing your classmates for the job you have created. Get as much information as you can to find the right person for the job.

useful questions

What kind of degree do you have?
What work experience do you have?
What hours can you work?
Do you mind . . . ?
Are you interested in . . . ?
Why should I hire you for the job?

C **GROUP WORK** Who would you hire for the job you posted? Why?

D **CLASS ACTIVITY** Compare the ideal jobs you created in part A. How are they similar? How are they different?

A List one movie, one TV show, one song, and one book.

B GROUP WORK Take turns making statements about each item.
Does everyone agree with each statement?

A: *Titanic* was filmed on a small lake in Mexico.
B: Are you sure? Wasn't it filmed on the ocean?
C: I'm pretty sure it was filmed in a plastic pool. I read it on the Internet.

C Now think of other famous creations and creators. Complete the chart.
Make some of the items true and some false.

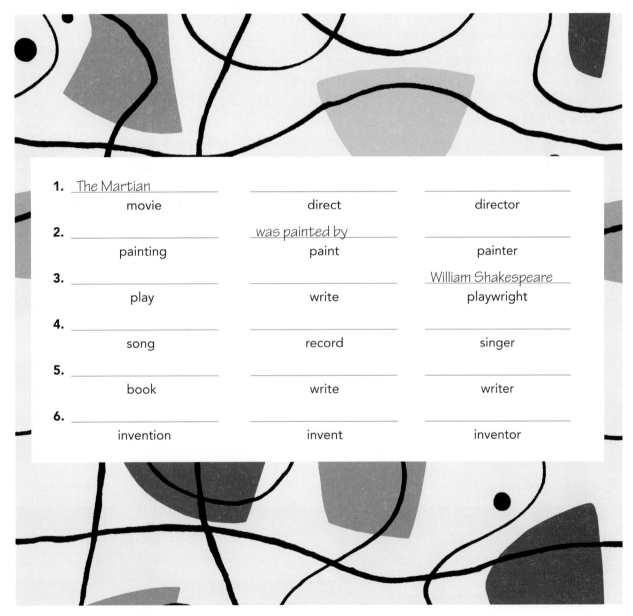

1. <u>The Martian</u> _____ _____
   movie   direct   director

2. _____ <u>was painted by</u> _____
   painting   paint   painter

3. _____ _____ <u>William Shakespeare</u>
   play   write   playwright

4. _____ _____ _____
   song   record   singer

5. _____ _____ _____
   book   write   writer

6. _____ _____ _____
   invention   invent   inventor

D GROUP WORK Make a statement about each item to your group members.
Ask them to decide which statements are true and which are false.

A: The movie *The Martian* was directed by Steven Spielberg.
B: I think that's true.
C: No, that's false. It was directed by Ridley Scott. I'm sure of it.

A GROUP WORK Play the board game. Follow these instructions.

1. Use small pieces of paper with your initials on them as markers.
2. Take turns tossing a coin:

 Move two spaces.   Move one space.

     Heads   **Tails**

3. Complete the sentence in the space you land on. Others ask two follow-up questions to get more information.

A: When I was little, I lived on the coast.
B: Oh, really? Did you go to the beach every day?
A: No, we only went to the beach on weekends.
C: Did you enjoy living there?

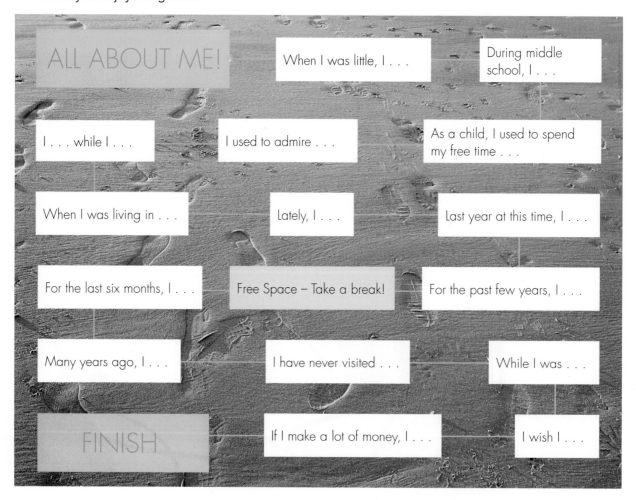

B CLASS ACTIVITY Tell the class an interesting fact that you learned about someone in your group.

"For the last six months, Marcia has been taking dance classes."

A Complete the questionnaire.

What is the name of a TV show or movie . . . ?

1. that made you laugh a lot

2. that made you feel sad

3. that you have seen more than once

4. which had great music

5. that was about a silly story

What is the name of a TV or movie star . . . ?

6. who is very talented

7. who is famous but not very talented

8. who does things to help society

9. who is an excellent comedian

10. that reminds you of someone you know

B PAIR WORK Compare your questionnaires. Ask follow-up questions of your own.

A: What's the name of a TV show or movie that made you laugh a lot?
B: *Grown Ups 2.*
A: Really? Why?
B: I thought the movie was hilarious.
A: Who was in it?
B: Adam Sandler. I always enjoy his movies.
A: Well, I liked his earlier movies better.

A PAIR WORK Look at this scene of an airport. What do you think is happening in each of the situations? Look at people's body language for clues.

A: Why do you think the couple in situation 1 looks upset?

B: Well, they might be having a fight. They look . . .

A: Who do you think the woman in situation 6 is?

B: She must be famous. She might . . .

B GROUP WORK Compare your interpretations. Do you agree or disagree?

Student A

A PAIR WORK You and your partner want to get together. Ask and answer questions to find a day when you are both free. You also want to keep time open for other friends, so give excuses for those days. Write your partner's excuses on the calendar.

A: Do you want to meet on the 2nd?
B: I'm sorry. I'm going to an engagement party. Are you free on the 1st?
A: Well, I . . .

Calendar						
Day	Week	**Month**	Year			
September					< Today >	
Sunday	Monday	Tuesday	Wednesday	Thursday	Friday	Saturday
					1 dinner with Pat	2
3	4 class	5	6	7 You want to keep this date free. Make an excuse.	8 party at Sam's	9
10	11 You want to keep this date free. Make an excuse.	12 bowling with Chris	13	14 movie with Haru	15	16
17 dinner with office friends	18 class	19	20	21 study for tomorrow's exam	22 You want to keep this date free. Make an excuse.	23
24	25	26 You want to keep these dates free. Make excuses.	27	28 dinner for Dad's birthday	29 go dancing with Jess & Bo	30 You might have a date. Give an excuse.

B PAIR WORK Now work with another student. Discuss the excuses your partner gave you in Part A. Decide which excuses were probably true and which ones were probably not true.

A: Pablo said that on the 7th he had to take care of his neighbors' cats. That was probably not true.
B: I agree. I think . . .

A What would you do in each of these situations? Circle **a**, **b**, or **c**.
If you think you would do something else, write your suggestion next to **d**.

1 If I saw someone shoplifting in a store, I would . . .
  a. pretend I didn't notice.
  b. talk to the store manager.
  c. talk to the shoplifter.
  d. _____.

2 If I saw an elderly woman trying to cross a street, I would . . .
  a. keep walking.
  b. offer to help.
  c. try to stop traffic for her.
  d. _____.

3 If I saw someone standing on a highway next to a car with smoke coming from the engine, I would . . .
  a. continue driving.
  b. stop and help.
  c. use my cell phone to call the police.
  d. _____.

4 If I saw my friend's boyfriend or girlfriend with someone other than my friend, I would . . .
  a. say nothing.
  b. talk to my friend.
  c. talk to my friend's boyfriend or girlfriend.
  d. _____.

5 If I were eating dinner in a restaurant and I found a hair in my food, I would . . .
  a. remove it and continue eating.
  b. mention it to the server.
  c. demand to speak to the manager.
  d. _____.

B GROUP WORK Compare your choices for each situation in part A.

A: What would you do if you saw someone shoplifting in a store?
B: I'm not sure. Maybe I would pretend I didn't notice.
C: Really? I wouldn't. I would . . .

C CLASS ACTIVITY Take a class survey. Find out which choice was most popular for each situation. Talk about any other suggestions people added for **d**.

Student B

A PAIR WORK You and your partner want to get together. Ask and answer questions to find a day when you are both free. You also want to keep time open for other friends, so give excuses for those days. Write your partner's excuses on the calendar.

A: Do you want to meet on the 2nd?
B: I'm sorry. I'm going to an engagement party. Are you free on the 1st?
A: Well, I . . .

Calendar

Day | Week | **Month** | Year

September

< | Today | >

Sunday	Monday	Tuesday	Wednesday	Thursday	Friday	Saturday
					1	2 Kelly's engagement party
3 You want to keep this date free. Make an excuse.	4 movie with Alex	5	6 You want to keep these dates free. Make excuses.	7	8	9
10 visit Mom and Dad	11 office party	12	13 photography workshop at school	14	15 You want to keep these dates free. Make excuses.	16
17 visit Grandma	18	19 jogging with Andie	20	21	22 party at Cameron's	23 dinner with Farah
24 family get-together	25 You need a break. Make an excuse.	26 study group meeting	27	28 work late: big report due Friday	29	30

B PAIR WORK Now work with another student. Discuss the excuses your partner gave you in Part A. Decide which excuses were probably true and which ones were probably not true.

A: Maria said that on the 9th she had to help her brother paint his kitchen. That might be true.
B: I agree. I think . . .

Grammar plus

UNIT 9

1 Time contrasts   page 59

■ Use the modal *might* to say something is possible in the present or future: In a few years, movie theaters **might** not exist. = In a few years, maybe movie theaters won't exist.

Complete the conversation with the correct form of the verbs in parentheses.
Use the past, present, or future tense.

A: I saw a fascinating program last night. It talked about the past, the present, and the future.

B: What kinds of things did it describe?

A: Well, for example, the normal work week in the 19th century _____ (be) over 60 hours. Nowadays, many people _____ (work) around 40 hours a week.

B: Well, that sounds like progress.

A: You're right. But on the show, they said that most people _____ (work) fewer hours in the future. They also talked about the way we shop. These days, many of us _____ (shop) online. In the old days, there _____ (be) no supermarkets, so people _____ (have to) go to a lot of different stores. In the future, people _____ (do) all their shopping from their phones.

B: I don't believe that.

A: Me neither. What about cars? Do you think people _____ (still drive) cars a hundred years from now?

B: What did they say on the show?

A: They said that before the car, people _____ (walk) everywhere. Nowadays, we _____ (drive) everywhere. And that _____ (not change).

2 Conditional sentences with *if* clauses   page 61

■ The *if* clause can come before or after the main clause: **If** I change my eating habits, I'll feel healthier./I'll feel healthier **if** I change my eating habits. Always use a comma when the *if* clause comes before the main clause.

■ For the future of *can*, use *will be able to*: If you save some money, you**'ll be able to buy** a car.
(NOT: . . . you'll can buy a car.)

■ For the future of *must*, use *will have to*: If you get a dog, you**'ll have to take care** of it.
(NOT: . . . you'll must take care of it.)

Complete the sentences with the correct form of the verbs in parentheses.

1. If you _____*exercise*_____ (exercise) more often, you'_ll feel_____ (feel) more energetic.

2. If you _____ (join) a gym, exercise _____ (become) part of your routine.

3. You _____ (not have to) worry about staying in shape if you _____ (work out) three or four times a week.

4. If you _____ (ride) a bike or _____ (run) a few times a week, you _____ (lose) weight and _____ (gain) muscle.

5. You _____ (sleep) better at night if you _____ (exercise) regularly.

6. If you _____ (start) exercising, you _____ (might/not have) as many colds and other health problems.

1 Gerunds; short responses page 65

> ■ Short responses with *so* and *neither* are ways of agreeing. The subject (noun or pronoun) comes after the verb: I love traveling. So **do I**. (NOT: So ~~I do~~.) I can't stand talking on the phone. Neither **can I**. (NOT: Neither ~~I can~~.)

Rewrite A's line using the words given. Then write an agreement for B.

1. I hate working alone. (can't stand)
   A: _I can't stand working alone._
   B: _Neither can I._

2. I don't like reading about politics or politicians. (interested in)
   A: _____
   B: _____

3. I can solve problems. (good at)
   A: _____
   B: _____

4. I have no problem with working on weekends. (don't mind)
   A: _____
   B: _____

5. I love learning new things. (enjoy)
   A: _____
   B: _____

6. I can't develop new ideas. (not good at)
   A: _____
   B: _____

2 Clauses with *because* page 68

> ■ Clauses with *because* answer the question "Why?" or "Why not?": Why would you make a good flight attendant? I'd make a good flight attendant **because** I love traveling, and I'm good with people.

Complete the sentences with *because* and the phrases in the box.

> I don't write very well
> I love arguing with people
> I'm afraid of flying
> ✓ I'm much too short
> I'm not patient enough to work with kids
> I'm really bad with numbers

1. I could never be a fashion model _because I'm much too short_____.
2. I wouldn't make a good high school teacher _____.
3. I wouldn't want to be a flight attendant _____.
4. I could never be an accountant _____.
5. I would make a bad journalist _____.
6. I'd be an excellent lawyer _____.

1 Passive with *by* (simple past)   page 73

- The past participle of regular verbs is the same form as the simple past: Leonardo da Vinci **painted** *Mona Lisa* in 1503. *Mona Lisa* was **painted** by Leonardo da Vinci in 1503.

- The past participle of some – but not all – irregular verbs is the same form as the simple past: The Egyptians **built** the Pyramids. The Pyramids were **built** by the Egyptians. BUT Jane Austen **wrote** *Pride and Prejudice*. *Pride and Prejudice* was **written** by Jane Austen.

Change the sentences from active to passive with *by*.

1. The Chinese invented paper around 100 C.E.
   Paper was invented by the Chinese around 100 C.E.

2. Marie Curie discovered radium in 1898.
_____

3. Dr. Felix Hoffmann made the first aspirin in 1899.
_____

4. Tim Berners-Lee developed the World Wide Web in 1989.
_____

5. William Herschel identified the planet Uranus in 1781.
_____

6. Georges Bizet wrote the opera *Carmen* in the 1870s.
_____

2 Passive without *by* (simple present)   page 75

- When it is obvious or not important who is doing the action, don't use a *by* phrase: Both the Olympics and the World Cup are held every four years. (NOT: . . . are held ~~by people~~ . . .)

Complete the information with *is* or *are* and the past participle of the verbs in the box.

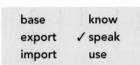

base	know
export	✓ speak
import	use

1. Portuguese – not Spanish – _is spoken_____ in Brazil.
2. Diamonds and gold from South Africa _____ by countries all over the world.
3. The U.S. dollar _____ in Puerto Rico.
4. Colombia _____ for its delicious coffee.
5. Many electronic products _____ by Japan and South Korea. It's an important industry for these two countries.
6. The economy in many island countries, such as Jamaica, _____ on tourism.

UNIT 12

1 Past continuous vs. simple past page 79

■ When the past continuous is used with the simple past, both actions happened at the same time, but the past continuous action started earlier. The simple past action interrupted the past continuous action.

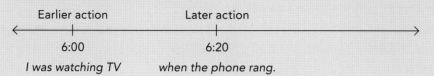

Earlier action   Later action

6:00   6:20

I was watching TV   *when the phone rang.*

Complete the conversations with the correct form of the verbs in parentheses.
Use the past continuous or the simple past.

1. **A:** What happened to you?
   B: I _____ *fell* _____ (fall) while I _____ *was jogging* _____ (jog) in the park.
2. **A:** _____ you _____ (see) the storm yesterday?
   B: Yes! It _____ (start) while I _____ (drive) to work.
3. **A:** We finally _____ (move) to a larger apartment.
   B: That's good. I know you _____ (live) in a tiny place when your daughter _____ (be) born.
4. **A:** My sister _____ (have) a bad accident. She _____ (hurt) her back when she _____ (lift) weights at the gym.
   B: That _____ (happen) to me last year, but I _____ (not lift) weights. I _____ (take) a boxing class, and I _____ (trip).

2 Present perfect continuous page 81

■ The same time expressions used with the present perfect can also be used with the present perfect continuous. Don't confuse *for* and *since*: I've been working here **for** 5 years./I've been working here **since** 2010.

Complete the sentences with the present perfect continuous form of the verbs in parentheses.

1. **A:** What _____ *have* _____ you _____ *been doing* _____ all day?
   B: I _____ (clean) the house, and Peter _____ (watch) TV.
   He _____ (not feel) very well lately.
   A: How _____ you _____ (feel) these days?
   B: I _____ (feel) great. I _____ (not eat) any junk food, and I _____ (exercise) a lot. I _____ (take) really good care of myself.
2. **A:** How long _____ you and Joe _____ (date)?
   B: We _____ (go out) together for almost a year. Can you believe it?
   A: Maya and I _____ (date) for even longer. I think it's time to get married. We _____ (talk) about it a lot lately.
   B: Joe and I _____ (not talk) about marriage, but I _____ (think) about it.

UNIT 13

1 Participles as adjectives *page 87*

■ Adjectives ending in *–ing* are present participles. They are things that *cause* a feeling.
Adjectives ending in *–ed* are past participles. They *express* the feeling.

Complete the sentences with the correct participle.

1. Why are we watching this _____*boring*_____ movie? Aren't you _____*bored*_____ with it? (boring / bored)

2. Kristen Stewart is an _____ actress. I'm _____ by her talent. (amazing / amazed)

3. Are you _____ in computer-generated special effects? The latest 3-D movies are very _____. (interesting / interested)

4. I had an _____ experience the last time I went to the movies. I started to cough, and I couldn't stop. I was really _____. (embarrassing / embarrassed)

5. Julie and I saw an Italian comedy yesterday. I found it _____, but Julie didn't seem very _____ by it. (amusing / amused)

6. Oh, I'm really _____ with Jeremy right now. He took me to the most _____ movie last night. I wanted to walk out after half an hour, but he wouldn't leave! (disgusting / disgusted)

7. Do you think sci-fi movie directors make their films _____ intentionally? I get so _____ by the complicated storylines and weird characters. (confusing / confused)

8. I think that great books make great movies. If I find a book _____, I'm usually _____ by the movie, too. (fascinating / fascinated)

2 Relative pronouns for people and things *page 89*

■ Relative clauses give information about nouns. Don't use a personal pronoun in a relative clause: He's an actor **that** won two Oscars. (NOT: He's an actor ~~that he won two Oscars.~~)

Complete the conversations. Use *that* for things and *who* for people.

A: How did you like the movie last night? Was it any good?

B: It wasn't bad, but it's not the kind of movie _____*that*_____ makes you think. I like films _____ have a strong message and interesting storylines.

A: How about the acting? Did you like the actors _____ star in it?

B: Jessica Biel is pretty good, actually.

A: Oh, she's that beautiful actress _____ is married to Justin Timberlake.

B: Justin who? Who's that?

A: Oh, you know him. He's the one _____ was in the band 'NSync years ago. It was a "boy band" _____ was popular in the 1990s.

B: I remember 'NSync, but I don't remember the names of the guys _____ were in the band.

A: Well, I loved Justin Timberlake when I was a kid. And he's not a bad actor. Did you see the movie *The Social Network*?

B: I did see that. It's about the guys _____ started Facebook, right? I didn't realize Justin Timberlake was in it. Now I'll have to see it again!

UNIT 14

1 Modals and adverbs page 93

> ■ Use the modals *might/may*, *could*, and *must* and the adverbs *maybe/perhaps*, *probably*, and *definitely* when you aren't sure about what you're saying:
> Slight possibility: *might, may, maybe, perhaps*
> Possibility: *could, probably*
> Strong possibility: *must, definitely*

Rewrite each sentence in different ways, using the words in parentheses.

1. Perhaps it means she doesn't agree with you.
    a. (maybe) _Maybe it means she doesn't agree with you._
    b. (might) _____
    c. (may) _____
2. That gesture could mean, "Come here."
    a. (probably) _____
3. That almost definitely means he doesn't understand you.
    a. (must) _____

2 Permission, obligation, and prohibition page 95

> ■ Use *have/has* with *got to*: You**'ve got to** keep the door closed. (NOT: You ~~got to~~ keep the door closed.)

Complete the conversations with the words and phrases in the box.
Use each word or phrase only once.

are allowed to	✓ **can't**
aren't allowed to	**have to**
can	**have got to**

1. A: Oh, no! That sign says, "No fishing." That means we
         _____can't_____ fish here.
    B: You're right. We _____ go somewhere else to fish. I
        think you _____ fish in the pond on Cedar Road. Let's go
        there.
2. A: What does that sign mean?
    B: It means bad news for us. It means you _____ bring dogs
        to the beach. We'd better take Buddy home.
3. A: Please don't leave your garbage here. You _____ put it
        in the trash room down the hall. That's one of the building's rules.
    B: I'm really sorry.
4. A: You _____ put your bike in the bike room downstairs, if
        you want. It's much safer than locking it up outside.
    B: Oh, that's great! I'll do that. I didn't know about the bike room.

1 Unreal conditional sentences with *if* clauses   page 101

■ The clauses in unreal conditional sentences can come in either order. Don't use a comma when the *if* clause comes second: **If** I won the lottery, I'd share the money with my family./I'd share the money with my family **if** I won the lottery.

Complete the conversation with the correct form of the verbs in parentheses.

1. A: If a friend _____ (ask) to borrow some money, what _____ you _____ (say)?

   B: Well, if I _____ (have) any extra money that month, I _____ probably _____ (give) it to her.

2. A: What _____ you _____ (do) if someone _____ (give) you a million dollars?

   B: Hmm, I'm not sure. I _____ (buy) a lot of nice clothes and jewelry, or I _____ (spend) some and _____ (give) some away, or I _____ (put) it all in the bank.

3. A: If you _____ (think) a friend was doing something dangerous, _____ you _____ (say) something to him, or _____ you _____ (keep) quiet?

   B: I _____ definitely _____ (talk) to my friend about it.

4. A: What _____ you _____ (do) if you _____ (have) a problem with your boss?

   B: That's a hard one. If that _____ (happen), I _____ (talk) to the human resources department about it, or I _____ just _____ (sit down) with my boss and _____ (talk) about the situation.

2 Past modals   page 103

■ Use *should have* and *would have* for all subjects. They don't change form: He **should have called** sooner. (NOT: He should has called sooner.)

Read the situations. Use the words in parentheses to write opinions and suggestions.

1. My neighbor had a party last night. It was very loud, so I called the police.
(you / speak / to your neighbor first)
   <u>You should have spoken to your neighbor first.</u>

2. The mail carrier put someone else's mail in my box. I threw it away.
(you / write / a note and leave / the mail in your box)

_____

3. My sister asked if I liked her new dress. It didn't look good on her, but I said it did.
(I / tell her the truth)

_____

4. A salesperson called me last night. I didn't want to buy anything, but I let her talk to me for almost half an hour.
(I / tell her I'm not interested / hang up)

_____

UNIT 16

1 Reported speech: requests page 107

■ When a reported request is negative, *not* comes before *to*: Don't leave your wet towel on the floor. She told me **not to leave** my wet towel on the floor.
(NOT: She told me ~~to not~~ leave my wet towel on the floor.)

Harry's roommate, Tyler, is making some requests. Read what Tyler said to Harry. Write the requests with the verbs in parentheses and reported speech.

1. "Can you put away your clean clothes?" (ask)
Tyler asked Harry to put away his clean clothes.

2. "Meet me in the cafeteria at school at noon." (say)

_____

3. "Don't leave your shoes in the living room." (tell)

_____

4. "Hang up your wet towels." (say)

_____

5. "Could you stop using my phone?" (ask)

_____

6. "Make your bed on weekdays." (tell)

_____

7. "Don't eat my food." (say)

_____

8. "Be a better roommate!" (tell)

_____

2 Reported speech: statements page 109

■ The tense of the introducing verb (*ask, say, tell*) changes when the sentence is reported: simple present → simple past; present continuous → past continuous; present perfect → past perfect. Modals change, too: *can* → *could*; *will* → *would*; *may* → *might*.

Bill and Kathy are having a barbecue on Sunday. They're upset because a lot of their friends can't come. Read what their friends said. Change the excuses into reported speech.

1. Lori: "I have to visit my grandparents that day."
Lori said that she had to visit her grandparents that day.

2. Mario: "I'm going to a play on Sunday."

_____

3. Julia: "I've promised to take my brother to the movies that day."

_____

4. Daniel: "I can't come. I have to study for a huge exam on Monday."

_____

5. The neighbors: "We'll be out of town all weekend."

_____

6. Alice: "I may have to babysit my nephew."

_____

Grammar plus answer key

Unit 9

1 Time contrasts

A: I saw a fascinating program last night. It talked about the past, the present, and the future.

B: What kinds of things did it describe?

A: Well, for example, the normal work week in the 19th century **was/used to be** over 60 hours. Nowadays, many people **work/are working** around 40 hours a week.

B: Well, that sounds like progress.

A: You're right. But on the show, they said that most people **will work/might work** fewer hours in the future. They also talked about the way we shop. These days, many of us **shop** online. In the old days, there **were** no supermarkets, so people **had to go/used to have to go** to a lot of different stores. In the future, people **will do/might do/are going to do** all their shopping from their phones.

B: I don't believe that.

A: Me neither. What about cars? Do you think people **will still drive/are still going to drive** cars a hundred years from now?

B: What did they say on the show?

A: They said that before the car, people **walked/used to walk** everywhere. Nowadays, we **drive** everywhere. And that **won't change/isn't going to change/'s not going to change**.

2 Conditional sentences with *if* clauses

2. If you **join** a gym, exercise **will become** part of your routine.
3. You **won't have to** worry about staying in shape if you **work out** three or four times a week.
4. If you **ride** a bike or **run** a few times a week, you**'ll lose** weight and **gain** muscle.
5. You**'ll sleep** better at night if you **exercise** regularly.
6. If you **start** exercising, you **might not have** as many colds and other health problems.

Unit 10

1 Gerunds; short responses

2. A: I'm not interested in reading about politics or politicians.
   B: Neither am I.
3. A: I'm good at solving problems.
   B: So am I.
4. A: I don't mind working on weekends.
   B: Neither do I.
5. A: I enjoy learning new things.
   B: So do I.
6. A: I'm not good at developing new ideas.
   B: Neither am I.

2 Clauses with *because*

2. I wouldn't make a good high school teacher **because I'm not patient enough to work with kids**.
3. I wouldn't want to be a flight attendant **because I'm afraid of flying**.
4. I could never be an accountant **because I'm really bad with numbers**.
5. I would make a bad journalist **because I don't write very well**.
6. I'd be an excellent lawyer **because I love arguing with people**.

Unit 11

1 Passive with *by* (simple past)

2. Radium was discovered by Marie Curie in 1898.
3. The first aspirin was made by Dr. Felix Hoffmann in 1899.
4. The World Wide Web was developed by Tim Berners-Lee in 1989.
5. The planet Uranus was identified in 1781 by William Herschel.
6. The opera *Carmen* was written by Georges Bizet in the 1870s.

2 Passive without *by* (simple present)

2. Diamonds and gold from South Africa **are imported** by countries all over the world.
3. The U.S. dollar **is used** in Puerto Rico.
4. Colombia **is known** for its delicious coffee.
5. Many electronic products **are exported** by Japan and Korea. It's an important industry for these two countries.
6. The economy in many island countries, such as Jamaica, **is based** on tourism.

Unit 12

1 Past continuous vs. simple past

2. A: **Did** you **see** the storm yesterday?
   B: Yes! It **started** while I **was driving** to work.
3. A: We finally **moved** to a larger apartment.
   B: That's good. I know you **were living** in a tiny place when your daughter **was** born.
4. A: My sister **had** a bad accident. She **hurt** her back when she **was lifting** weights at the gym.
   B: That **happened** to me last year, but I **wasn't lifting** weights. I **was taking** a boxing class, and I **tripped**.

2 Present perfect continuous

1. A: What **have** you **been doing** all day?
   B: I**'ve been cleaning** the house, and Peter **has been watching** TV. He **hasn't been feeling** very well lately.
   A: How **have** you **been feeling** these days?
   B: I**'ve been feeling** great. I **haven't been eating** any junk food, and I**'ve been exercising** a lot. I**'ve been taking** really good care of myself.
2. A: How long **have** you and Joe **been dating**?
   B: We**'ve been going out** together for almost a year. Can you believe it?
   A: Maya and I **have been dating** for even longer. I think it's time to get married. We**'ve been talking** about it a lot lately.
   B: Joe and I **haven't been talking** about marriage, but I**'ve been thinking** about it.

Unit 13

1 Participles as adjectives

2. Kristen Stewart is an **amazing** actress. I'm **amazed** by her talent.
3. Are you **interested** in computer-generated special effects? The latest 3-D movies are very **interesting**.
4. I had an **embarrassing** experience the last time I went to the movies. I started to cough, and I couldn't stop. I was really **embarrassed**.
5. Julie and I saw an Italian comedy yesterday. I found it **amusing**, but Julie didn't seem very **amused** by it.
6. Oh, I'm really **disgusted** with Jeremy right now. He took me to the most **disgusting** movie last night. I wanted to walk out after half an hour, but he wouldn't leave!
7. Do you think sci-fi movie directors make their films **confusing** intentionally? I get so **confused** by the complicated storylines and weird characters.
8. I think that great books make great movies. If I find a book **fascinating**, I'm usually **fascinated** by the movie, too.

2 Relative pronouns for people and things

A: How did you like the movie last night? Was it any good?
B: It wasn't bad, but it's not the kind of movie **that** makes you think. I like films **that** have a strong message and interesting storylines.
A: How about the acting? Did you like the actors **who** star in it?
B: Jessica Biel is pretty good, actually.
A: Oh, she's that beautiful actress **who** is married to Justin Timberlake.
B: Justin who? Who's that?
A: Oh, you know him. He's the one **who** was in the band 'NSync years ago. It was a "boy band" **that** was popular in the 1990s.
B: I remember 'NSync, but I don't remember the names of the guys **who** were in the band.
A: Well, I loved Justin Timberlake when I was a kid. And he's not a bad actor. Did you see the movie *The Social Network*?
B: I did see that. It's about the guys **who** started Facebook, right? I didn't realize Justin Timberlake was in it. Now I'll have to see it again!

Unit 14

1 Modals and adverbs

1. a. Maybe it means she doesn't agree with you.
   b. It might mean she doesn't agree with you.
   c. It may mean she doesn't agree with you.
2. a. That gesture probably means, "Come here."
3. a. That must mean he doesn't understand you.

2 Permission, obligation, and prohibition

1. A: Oh, no! That sign says, "No fishing." That means we **can't** fish here.
   B: You're right. We**'ve got to/have to** go somewhere else to fish. I think you**'re allowed to/can** fish in the pond on Cedar Road. Let's go there.
2. A: What does that sign mean?
   B: It means bad news for us. It means you **aren't allowed to** bring dogs to the beach. We'd better take Buddy home.
3. A: Please don't leave your garbage here. You**'ve got to/ have to** put it in the trash room down the hall. That's one of the building's rules.
   B: I'm really sorry.
4. A: You **can** put your bike in the bike room downstairs, if you want. It's much safer than locking it up outside.
   B: Oh, that's great! I'll do that. I didn't know about the bike room.

Unit 15

1 Unreal conditional sentences with *if* clauses

1. A: If a friend **asked** to borrow some money, what **would** you **say**?
   B: Well, if I **had** any extra money that month, I **would** probably **give** it to her.
2. A: What **would/could** you **do** if someone **gave** you a million dollars?
   B: Hmm, I'm not sure. I **could/might buy** a lot of nice clothes and jewelry, or I **could/might spend** some and **give** some away, or I **could/might put** it all in the bank.
3. A: If you **thought** a friend was doing something dangerous, **would** you **say** something to him, or **would** you **keep** quiet?
   B: I **would** definitely **talk** to my friend about it.
4. A: What **would** you **do** if you **had** a problem with your boss?
   B: That's a hard one. If that **happened**, I **might/could talk** to the human resources department about it, or I **might/ could** just **sit down** with my boss and **talk** about the situation.

2 Past modals

2. You should have written a note and left the mail in your box.
3. I would have told her the truth.
4. I would have told her I wasn't interested and hung up (the phone).

Unit 16

1 Reported speech: requests

2. Tyler said to meet him in the cafeteria at school at noon.
3. Tyler told him/Harry not to leave his shoes in the living room.
4. Tyler said to hang up his wet towels.
5. Tyler asked him/Harry to stop using his/Tyler's phone.
6. Tyler told him/Harry to make his bed on weekdays.
7. Tyler said not to eat his/Tyler's food.
8. Tyler told him/Harry to be a better roommate.

2 Reported speech: statements

1. Lori said (that) she had to visit her grandparents that day.
   Lori told them (that) she had to visit her grandparents that day.
2. Mario said/told them (that) he was going to a play on Sunday.
3. Julia said/told them (that) she had promised to take her brother to the movies that day.
4. Daniel said/told them (that) he couldn't come because he had to study for a huge exam on Monday.
5. The neighbors said/told them (that) they would be out of town all weekend.
6. Alice said/told them (that) she might have to babysit her nephew.

Credits

The authors and publishers acknowledge the following sources of copyright material and are grateful for the permissions granted. While every effort has been made, it has not always been possible to identify the sources of all the material used, or to trace all copyright holders. If any omissions are brought to our notice, we will be happy to include the appropriate acknowledgements on reprinting and in the next update to the digital edition, as applicable.

Texts

Text on p. 83 adapted from "Deaf band 'Beethoven's Nightmare' feels the music" by Dennis McCarthy. Copyright © Los Angeles Daily News. Reproduced with permission.

Key: B = Below, BC = Below Centre, BL = Below Left, BR = Below Right, B/G = Background, C = Centre, CL = Centre Left, CR = Centre Right, L = Left, R = Right, T = Top, TC = Top Centre, TL = Top Left, TR = Top Right.

Illustrations

337 Jon (KJA Artists): 39, 92(B), 97; **Mark Duffin**: 18, 25(C), 37, 43(T); **Pablo Gallego** (Beehive Illustration): 43(B); **Thomas Girard** (Good Illustration): 2, 22, 41, 93; **John Goodwin** (Eye Candy Illustration): 40; **Daniel Gray**: 75, 118, 120; **Quino Marin** (The Organisation): 36, 80, 128; **Gavin Reece** (New Division): 58, 81, 119; **Paul Williams** (Sylvie Poggio Artists): 16, 114.

Photos

Back cover (woman with whiteboard): Jenny Acheson/Stockbyte/GettyImages; Back cover (whiteboard): Nemida/GettyImages; Back cover (man using phone): Betsie Van Der Meer/Taxi/GettyImages; Back cover (woman smiling): PeopleImages.com/DigitalVision/GettyImages; Back cover (name tag): Tetra Images/GettyImages; Back cover (handshake): David Lees/Taxi/GettyImages; p. v (TL): Hero Images/Getty Images; p. v (TR): Cultura RM Exclusive/dotdotred/Getty Images; p. v (CL): vitchanan/iStock/Getty Images Plus/Getty Images; p. v (CR): Svetlana Braun/iStock/Getty Images Plus/Getty Images; p. v (BL): Hero Images/Getty Images; p. v (BR): Cultura RM Exclusive/dotdotred/Getty Images; p. vi (Unit 9), p. 58 (header): Artur Debat/Moment/Getty Images; p. 58 (TL): Michael Fresco/Evening Standard/Hulton Archive/Getty Images; p. 58 (TC): Car Culture/Car Culture ® Collection/Getty Images; p. 58 (TR): Javier Pierini/The Image Bank/Getty Images; p. 59: Hero Images/Getty Images; p. 60 (CR): Jordan Siemens/Iconica/Getty Images; p. 60 (BR): RoBeDeRo/E+/Getty Images; p. 61: GH-Photography/iStock/Getty Images Plus/Getty Images; p. 62 (TR): Barry Austin Photography/Iconica/Getty Images; p. 62 (Ex 11a: photo 1): Hill Street Studios/Blend Images/Getty Images; p. 62 (Ex 11a: photo 2): Hill Street Studios/Blend Images/Getty Images; p. 62 (Ex 11a: photo 3): Hill Street Studios/Blend Images/Getty Images; p. 62 (Ex 11a: photo 4): Aziz Ary Neto/Cultura/Getty Images; p. 62 (Ex 11a: photo 5): Blend Images-Mike Kemp/Brand X Pictures/Getty Images; p. 63: Daniel Schoenen/LOOK-foto/LOOK/Getty Images; p. vi (Unit 10), p. 64 (header): Hero Images/Getty Images; p. 64 (BR): BJI/Blue Jean Images/Getty Images; p. 65: Caiaimage/Paul Bradbury/Caiaimage/Getty Images; p. 67 (disorganised): Stuart McCall/Photographer's Choice/Getty Images; p. 67 (hardworking): Dave and Les Jacobs/Blend Images/Getty Images; p. 67 (Ex 9a): adventtr/E+/Getty Images; p. 67 (Paula): Portra Images/Taxi/Getty Images; p. 67 (Shawn): PeopleImages/DigitalVision/Getty Images; p. 67 (Dalia): Jetta Productions/Blend Images/Getty Images; p. 68: Hill Street Studios/Getty Images; p. 69: Image Source/Getty Images; p. 71: monkeybusinessimages/iStock/Getty Images Plus/Getty Images; p. vi (Unit 11), p. 72 (header): d3sign/Moment/Getty Images; p. 72 (Eiffel Tower): Kart Thomas/Photolibrary/Getty Images; p. 72 (Machu Picchu): mimmopellicola.com/Moment/Getty Images; p. 72 (Neuschwanstein Castle): Brian Lawrence/Getty Images; p. 72 (Mount Fuji): Christian Kober/robertharding/Getty Images; p. 72 (Statue of Liberty): Brian Lawrence/Getty Images; p. 72 (Big Ben): Joe Fox/Photographer's Choice/Getty Images; p. 73: Print Collector/Hulton Fine Art Collection/Getty Images; p. 74 (L): JTB Photo/Universal Images Group/Getty Images; p. 74 (C): PIERRE VERDY/AFP Creative/Getty Images; p. 74 (R): JLGutierrez/iStock/Getty Images Plus/Getty Images; p. 76 (TR): Radius Images/Getty Images Plus/Getty Images; p. 76 (CR): Jodi Jacobson/E+/Getty Images; p. 76 (BR): Photography Aubrey Stoll/Moment/Getty Images; p. 77 (TL): Hemant Chawla/The India Today Group/Getty Images; p. 77 (CR): Luis Javier Sandoval/Oxford Scientific/Getty Images; p. 77 (BL): EPA european pressphoto agency b.v./Alamy; p. vi (Unit 12), p. 78 (header): Timur Emek/Getty Images Europe/Getty Images; p. 78 (TL): JasnaXX/RooM/Getty Images; p. 78 (TR): Rodrigo Alvarez-Icaza/Moment Open/Getty Images; p. 78 (BR): James Woodson/Photodisc/Getty Images; p. 79 (TR): Michael Krinke/Vetta/Getty Images; p. 79 (BR): biglike/iStock/Getty Images Plus/Getty Images; p. 82: David Lees/Taxi/Getty Images; p. 83: Rachel Murray/WireImage/Getty Images; p. 84: Ben Pruchnie/Getty Images Europe/Getty Images; p. vi (Unit 13), p. 86 (header): spawns/iStock/Getty Images Plus/Getty Images; p. 86 (TL): Jim Spellman/WireImage/Getty Images; p. 86 (TR): Pictorial Press Ltd/Alamy; p. 86 (BR): Murray Close/Contributor/Moviepix/GettyImages; p. 87: Araya Diaz/WireImage/Getty Image; p. 89: Jon Kopaloff/FilmMagic/Getty Images; p. 90 (TR): Daniel Zuchnik/WireImage/Getty Images; p. 90 (BR): Valerie Macon/Getty Images North America/Getty Images; p. 91 (BL): Paul Hawthorne/Getty Images North America/Getty Images; p. 91 (TR): Alberto E. Rodriguez/Getty Images North America/Getty Images; p. vi (Unit 14), p. 92 (header): Joe Drivas/Photographer's Choice/Getty Images; p. 93 (Ex 4: photo 1): champja/iStock/Getty Images Plus/Getty Images; p. 93 (Ex 4: photo 2): Dahl Per/Getty Images; p. 93 (Ex 4: photo 3): Seymour Hewitt/The Image Bank/Getty Images; p. 93 (Ex 4: photo 4): Merbe/E+/Getty Images; p. 93 (Ex 4: photo 5): BJI/Blue Jean Images/Getty Images; p. 93 (Ex 4: photo 6): m-imagephotography/iStock/Getty Images Plus/Getty Images; p. 94: BJI/Blue Jean Images/Getty Images; p. 98: uniquely india/Getty Images; p. 99: GlobalStock/E+/Getty Images; p. vi (Unit 15), p. 100 (header): Tetra Images/Getty Images; p. 100 (TL): moodboard/Brand X Pictures/Getty Images; p. 100 (CL): Marcin Balcerzak/Hemera/Getty Images Plus/Getty Images; p. 100 (C): Erik Dreyer/The Image Bank/Getty Images; p. 100 (BR): Thomas_EyeDesign/E+/Getty Images; p. 102: pp76/iStock/Getty Images Plus/Getty Images; p. 104 (TR): Wavebreakmedia Ltd/Wavebreak Media/Getty Images Plus/Getty Images; p. 104 (CR): Ariel Skelley/Blend Images/Getty Images Plus/Getty Images; p. 105 (Jack): Frank Herholdt/The Image Bank/Getty Images; p. 105 (Sarah): Betsie Van Der Meer/Taxi/Getty Images; p. 105 (Maya): Caiaimage/Sam Edwards/Caiaimage/Getty Images; p. 105 (Dag): Dimitri Otis/Taxi/Getty Images; p. 105 (Andres): Ridofranz/iStock/Getty Images Plus/Getty Images; p. 105 (Marta): Mark Edward Atkinson/Tracey Lee/Blend Images/Getty Images; p. vi (Unit 16), p. 106 (header): Dan Dumitru Comaniciu/iStock/Getty Images Plus/Getty Images; p. 106 (TR): GK Hart/Vikki Hart/Stone/Getty Images; p. 107: ajr_images/iStock/Getty Images Plus/Getty Images; p. 108 (Gabriel): gradyreese/E+/Getty Images; p. 108 (Craig): Leland Bobbe/Image Source/Getty Images; p. 109 (Grant): Ezra Bailey/Taxi/Getty Images; p. 109 (Sayo): Sappington Todd/Getty Images; p. 109 (Diego): Fuse/Getty Images; p. 109 (Carrie): Jordan Siemens/Getty Images; p. 110: Jamie Grill/Photodisc/Getty Images; p. 111 (TR): Tom Le Goff/DigitalVision/Getty Images; p. 111 (CR): Ugurhan Betin/iStock/Getty Images Plus/Getty Images; p. 112: Moodboard Stock Photography Ltd./Canopy/Getty Images; p. 123 (Ex a.1): Hero Images/Getty Images; p. 123 (Ex a.2): Kontrec/E+/Getty Images; p. 123 (Ex a.3): Robert Daly/Caiaimage/Getty Images; p. 123 (Ex a.4): quavondo/E+/Getty Images; p. 123 (Ex a.5): Wavebreakmedia Ltd/Wavebreak Media/Getty Images Plus/Getty Images; p. 123 (Ex a.6): Wendy Connett/Moment/Getty Images; p. 123 (Ex a.7): Dimitri Otis/DigitalVision/Getty Images; p. 123 (Ex a.8): Justin Pumfrey/Iconica/Getty Images; p. 123 (Ex a.9): monkeybusinessimages/iStock/Getty Images Plus/Getty Images; p. 123 (Ex a.10): Alberto Guglielmi/The Image Bank/Getty Images; p. 124: opolja/iStock/Getty Images Plus/Getty Images; p. 125 (B/G): CSA Images/Printstock Collection/Getty Images; p. 126 (TL): blackred/E+/Getty Images; p. 126 (TR): blackred/E+/Getty Images; p. 126 (B/G): Nathaniel Newbold/EyeEm/Getty Images; p. 127: JGI/Tom Grill/Blend Images/Getty Images; p. 130: Joos Mind/Taxi/Getty Images.

interchange

FIFTH EDITION

Video Activity Worksheets

2 B

Jack C. Richards
Revised by Lynne Robertson

CAMBRIDGE
UNIVERSITY PRESS

Credits

Plan of Video 2B

Car, bike, or bus?

☰ Preview

1 CULTURE

The first vehicle similar to a bicycle was built in 1690 in France. It was called a hobbyhorse. In Scotland, in 1840, pedals were added and it became the first real bicycle. Today there are twice as many bicycles as cars. There are over a billion bicycles in the world, with 400 million of them in China alone. In the U.S., almost 90 universities now have a campus bike program. Students "check out" the bikes to get around campus. This helps cut down on traffic, reduce pollution, and improve campus safety, but students need to remember: The bikes still need to be locked!

Do people ride bicycles in your country? How about 25 years ago?
How do people travel now?
Do most people own a car? How about a bicycle?

2 VOCABULARY Transportation costs

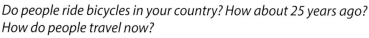

A **PAIR WORK** Do you know all of these words? Circle the word in each item that doesn't belong.

1. car   insurance   parking ticket   (sidewalk)

2. tires   expense   bicycle   helmet

3. job   loan   credit   debt

4. repairs   bus   route   public transportation

5. lend   commute   borrow   manage

B Now choose two words from each item and use them in a sentence, like this:

"I bought a new car, but then I couldn't afford the insurance!"

3 GUESS THE STORY

Look at the characters. Which form of transportation do you think each one prefers? Write it on the line.

> bike   car   bus

1. Luis

....

2. Jessica

....

3. Will

....

4. Emi

....

☰ Watch the video

4 GET THE PICTURE

A Look at your answers to Exercise 3. Did you guess correctly? Write the transportation each person prefers in the chart.

	Luis	Jessica	Will	Emi
Transportation:	car	....	....	....
Other:	can take out a car loan	....	....	....

B Now write one more piece of information about each person. Compare with a partner.

5 WATCH FOR DETAILS

Check (✓) **True** or **False**. Then correct the false statements. Compare with a partner.

	True	False	
1. Luis rides a bike now.	☐	✓	Luis takes the bus now.
2. Luis has already told his wife about the car.	☐	☐	....
3. Will rode his bike through a puddle.	☐	☐	....
4. Jessica will drive to work after graduation.	☐	☐	....
5. A car loan can help someone establish credit.	☐	☐	....
6. Someone else bought the car Luis wants.	☐	☐	....

6 WHAT'S YOUR OPINION?

A Complete the sentences with the consequences you think will happen.

1. If you buy a car before you have a job, ...

2. If you take out a car loan, ...

3. If you ride a bike instead of driving, ...

4. If you take the bus to work, ...

5. If you walk everywhere you go, ...

6. If you're not careful where you park your car, ...

B **PAIR WORK** Choose three sentences from part A and share your opinions.

Follow-up

7 YOUR CITY

A **PAIR WORK** In your city or town, what are the advantages and disadvantages of these forms of transportation? Complete the chart. Then compare around the class.

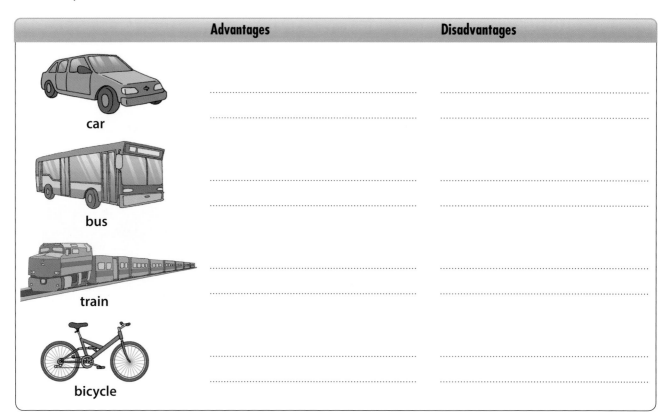

	Advantages	Disadvantages
car		
bus		
train		
bicycle		

B Convince another pair to leave their cars at home. Give as many reasons as you can why another form of transportation is better.

"If you drive a car every day, you're going to spend a lot of money on gas."

8 WHAT DID THEY SAY?

Watch the video and complete the conversation. Then practice it.

Jessica and Will warn Luis about the expenses of owning a car.

Jessica: People ....*used*.... ....*to*.... pay for things with cash. They
didn't buy on credit. ....
money to buy the car, you're ....
.... that debt for years.

Will: And even .... you .... the debt,
you're going to have to spend a lot of .... on the car.
You're going to .... to pay for ....
insurance, and you're going to .... to pay for
....

Jessica: Yeah, and you're going to have to pay for ....
And, if you're not .... , you're going to pay
parking .... It all ....

Luis: You're right. I didn't think .... the expenses.

Jessica: After graduation, I'm still going to ....
.... to work. But that's OK with me. Public transportation
in .... city is .... efficient.

9 TALKING ABOUT THE PAST, PRESENT, AND FUTURE

A Complete each sentence with at least two of the phrases
in the box. Then compare with a partner.

In the past, people used to . . .

1. ....
2. ....

Today, many people . . .

3. ....
4. ....

In the future, people will . . .

5. ....
6. ....

think it's safer to get a job before
    you buy a car
pay for things with cash
take the bus to work
not buy things on credit
establish credit through loans
walk or bike to work more often

B Write two more sentences of your own about transportation in the
past, present, and future. Take turns reading them to a partner.

1. ....
2. ....

The job interview

1 CULTURE

Nearly 50 percent of North American college students have an internship at some point during college. In Canada, internships are called *co-ops*. A co-op, or internship, is like a temporary job, usually related to the student's major. Internships often take place during the summer when students are not in school. Others may be part-time during the school year. Some colleges offer course credit for doing an internship, and some employers pay interns a small wage. All internships allow students to gain experience in a new field. Interning is a great way to break into a company because employers often hire the former interns after they graduate.

Have you ever had a part-time job or internship? What did you do? Where would you like to work?

2 VOCABULARY *Getting a job*

PAIR WORK What questions would a job interviewer ask at a fast-food restaurant? Match the parts of the sentences. Then add two questions of your own.

1. Where did you   want to work here?
2. What are your   find out about this job?
3. Why do you   well with children?
4. Do you like   qualifications?
5. Do you get along   good with money?
6. Are you   working with people?

7. ....

8. ....

3 GUESS THE STORY

PAIR WORK What do you think each job candidate is like? Write a few words for each person.

Susan	Scott
professional	....
....	....

Susan

Scott

Watch the video

4 GET THE PICTURE

Complete the sentences. Then compare with a partner.

1. Mario Verdi is the ....
2. Danielle Derby is the ....
3. Susan and Scott are applying for an ....
4. Susan is quite skilled with ....
5. Scott enjoys working with ....
6. Mario likes .... Danielle prefers ....

5 WHO SAID WHAT?

A Who said the sentences below? Check (✓) the correct answers. Then compare with a partner.

	Danielle	Susan	Scott	Mario
1. I know all of the main design programs.	☐	✓	☐	☐
2. Would you be able to create a banner ad for a web page?	☐	☐	☐	☐
3. I love sports, and I love marketing.	☐	☐	☐	☐
4. I see you're quite skilled with computers.	☐	☐	☐	☐
5. Do you have any sales experience?	☐	☐	☐	☐
6. I can sell anything.	☐	☐	☐	☐
7. I love being busy.	☐	☐	☐	☐
8. I don't mind trying new things because I'm a very fast learner.	☐	☐	☐	☐

6 WHAT'S YOUR OPINION?

A What skills does the internship require? Write two more skills in the chart.

Job skills	Susan	Scott
Design skills	☐	☐
Computer skills	☐	☐
Other:	☐	☐
Other:	☐	☐

B Does Susan have the skills? Does Scott have the skills? Check (✓) the correct answers.

C (PAIR WORK) Discuss who you think is best for the job and why.

A: I think Scott has more of the skills the job needs. He said he's good with numbers.

B: Oh, I don't think so. I think when he says he's good at computers, he's exaggerating.

☰ Follow-up

7 INTERVIEW

(PAIR WORK) Interview a classmate for an internship. Use the questions in Exercise 2 and in the video to help you. Start like this:

A: Why do you want an internship here?

B: Well, I'm very creative. . . .

8 JOB SKILLS

A (PAIR WORK) What do a salesperson and a graphic designer need to be good at? Choose from these phrases and add other ideas of your own.

managing money
solving problems
using computers

using their visual sense
getting along with people

B (GROUP WORK) Now play a game. What skills do people with these jobs need? Take turns giving your ideas. Think of as many things as you can. The person with the most ideas wins.

a chef   a firefighter   a teacher

C What are you good at? Tell your group. Your classmates will suggest an appropriate career for you!

**A manager needs to be good
at managing money.**

Interchange VRB 2 © Cambridge University Press 2012   Photocopiable

Language close-up

9 WHAT DID THEY SAY?

Watch the video and complete the conversation. Then practice it.

Danielle and Mario interview an internship candidate.

Mario: You have a very ....impressive.... résumé, Susan. .... us about ....

Susan: Well, Mr. Verdi, I'm .... and I .... that my artistic .... would .... well here.

Danielle: I see you're quite .... with ....

Susan: Yes. I .... all the .... design .... And I'm actually .... a .... for my father's .... , and I'm .... a 3-D software .... this ....

Danielle: Excellent! But won't you be .... for an internship?

Susan: Oh, no. I .... busy.

10 SHORT RESPONSES *Giving personal information*

A Write personal responses to these statements, choosing from the expressions below. Then compare with a partner.

So am I.	Neither am I.	I am.	I'm not.
So do I.	Neither do I.	I do.	I don't.
So can I.	Neither can I.	I can.	I can't.

1. I like working with numbers. ....

2. I enjoy working with computers. ....

3. I'm not good at managing money. ....

4. I don't like doing office work. ....

5. I can sell anything. ....

6. I can't type very fast. ....

I can design an ad.

So can I.

B Now write four new statements about yourself and read them to your partner. Your partner will respond with one of the expressions above.

1. .... 3. ....

2. .... 4. ....

11 Two brothers in Peru

≡ Preview

1 CULTURE

Peru is located in western South America. It is bordered by the Pacific coast, divided by the Andes Mountains, and is partly covered by the Amazon Rain Forest. Nearly 30 million people live in this diverse land. Spanish is the official language, but many people speak the native language, Quechua. Peru is the home of Machu Picchu, an archaeological site that once was a busy Incan city. It was abandoned about 500 years ago but is now a popular destination for tourists, historians, and hikers. Machu Picchu is a UNESCO World Heritage site and an important cultural attraction.

Would you like to visit Machu Picchu? Why or why not?
What do you enjoy most about traveling?

2 VOCABULARY Sightseeing

A **PAIR WORK** What can you do when you travel to a historic site? Put the words in the chart. Can you add two more words?

| ✓ancient ruins | go hiking | join a tour group | temples |
| eat at restaurants | hot springs | shop at local markets | |

Things to see	Things to do
ancient ruins	

B Which things in your chart do you like to do the most?

3 GUESS THE FACTS

Watch the first 30 seconds of the video with the sound off.
Answer these questions.

Who are the people in the video?
What do you think the video is going to show?

Interchange VRB 2 © Cambridge University Press 2012   Photocopiable

4 GET THE PICTURE

A These are the things that Derek and Paul did in Peru. Put the pictures in order (1 to 5).

B Now write the correct sentence under each picture. Compare with a partner.

They climbed Huayna Picchu for a different view.
They saw the Incas' "riding lawnmower," the llama.
They ate fruits and vegetables from local markets.

They took the train back to Cusco.
✓ They hiked the Inca Trail to Machu Picchu.

....

....

....

....

They hiked the Inca Trail to
Machu Picchu.

....

....

....

....

5 WHAT'S YOUR OPINION?

A What do you think of Derek and Paul's trip? Rate each part of the trip from 1 (very interesting) to 5 (not interesting). Circle the numbers.

1. Exploring Machu Picchu	1	2	3	4	5
2. Visiting the town of Aguas Calientes	1	2	3	4	5
3. Seeing the open market with fruits and vegetables	1	2	3	4	5
4. Learning about the history of Machu Picchu	1	2	3	4	5
5. Climbing Huayna Picchu	1	2	3	4	5

B **PAIR WORK** Compare opinions.

A: What did you think of exploring Machu Picchu?   B: It looked fun. I gave it a 1. How about you? . . .

6 WATCH FOR DETAILS

Write one thing that you learned about the people, places, or things below. Then compare with a partner.

1. Machu Picchu ....

2. The Inca ....

3. Aguas Calientes ....

4. Huayna Picchu ....

5. Paul and Derek ....

Follow-up

7 A DAY AT MACHU PICCHU

A GROUP WORK Use your knowledge of Machu Picchu to plan three things to do. Choose from the suggestions in the tourist brochure below.

Bus or hike to Machu Picchu.

Join a tour of Machu Picchu.

Learn about the history of Hiram Bingham and the site.

See llamas.

Explore and shop in the local markets.

Hike to Huayna Picchu.

Start like this:

A: I'd like to learn about Hiram Bingham.
B: So would I. I wonder what year he was born. . . .

B CLASS ACTIVITY Compare answers as a class.

Language close-up

8 *WHAT DID HE SAY?*

Watch the video and complete the description. Then compare with a partner.

Paul talks about the construction of Machu Picchu.

Machu Picchu, which means "Old Peak," ....was.... ....constructed....
around 1450. .... , as the empire collapsed ....
the Spanish, it .... abandoned, roughly 100 years
.... Machu Picchu ....
the outside ....

In 1911, the site .... explorer
and historian Hiram Bingham .... the ....
of some .... residents. He .... the
.... job of clearing .... hundreds of
.... of .... growth from the ....

9 *THE PASSIVE* *Giving factual information*

A Imagine that Paul and Derek said these things about Machu Picchu.
Complete the sentences using the verbs in parentheses.
Then compare with a partner.

1. The historic site of Machu Picchu ....is located.......... in Peru. (locate)
2. Tourists .... all the comforts of home in Aguas Calientes. (offer)
3. This entire hotel .... out by tourists. (rent)
4. Ancient techniques .... still .... by craftsmen in this town. (use)
5. The buildings .... out of blocks of stone. (build)
6. The site .... by half a million people a year! (visit)

B Now write five sentences about your own city using the passive. Compare around the class.

1. ....
2. ....
3. ....
4. ....
5. ....

Profile: A TV reporter

1 CULTURE

Changes in technology have changed journalism. News media have shifted from the printed word of newspapers and magazines to the Internet. Reporters still report on current events, but on the Internet, stories often include photos, videos, and frequent updates throughout the day. Today, a reporter can carry his or her own video camera or even report using a cell phone. And as more readers are posting their own news stories and opinions online, the face of journalism is changing.

Where do you get your news?
What do you think is the biggest change to journalism today?
How do you think journalism will change in the next 10 years?

2 VOCABULARY *The life of a reporter*

PAIR WORK Put the words in the word map.

✓ car accident	house fire	learning a language	radio reporter	TV reporter
corruption	laptop computer	organized crime	riding a bike	video camera

Types of reporters
....
....

Technology to produce stories
....
....

The Life of a Reporter

Story assignments
car accident
....
....
....

Hobbies
....
....

3 GUESS THE FACTS

Watch the first minute and a half of the video with the sound off.
Answer these questions.

1. Where do you think this person works?

   ....

2. Where do you think he lives?

   ....

3. What hobbies do you think he has?

   ....

☰ Watch the video

4 GET THE PICTURE

Look at your answers to Exercise 3. Did you guess correctly? Correct your
answers. Then compare with a partner.

5 WATCH FOR DETAILS

Check (✓) **True** or **False**. Then correct the false statements. Compare with a partner.

	True	False	
1. Kai Nagata owns the Canadian Broadcasting Company (CBC).	☐	✓	<u>Kai works for the CBC.</u>
2. The CBC news network is in Canada.	☐	☐	....
3. When Kai first moved to Montreal, he spoke French very well.	☐	☐	....
4. Kai started out as a TV reporter.	☐	☐	....
5. Kai tells his stories in words.	☐	☐	....
6. Kai uses a laptop computer to produce stories.	☐	☐	....
7. Kai wants to tell stories about other countries.	☐	☐	....
8. Lately, Kai has been assigned to stories about corruption.	☐	☐	....
9. Kai likes knowing what stories he'll be assigned.	☐	☐	....
10. Kai thinks he will be a journalist for a short time.	☐	☐	....

6 WHAT'S YOUR OPINION?

A (PAIR WORK) What stories has Kai Nagata covered? Check (✓) your answers. Can you add one or two more stories that you heard mentioned? Then compare with a partner.

☐ corruption

☐ demonstration

☐ house fire

☐ ....

☐ inflation

☐ ....

B If you were a reporter, which stories in part A would you like to cover? Which wouldn't you like to cover? Think of two more stories you would like to cover. Write them below. Discuss with a partner.

1. ....   2. ....

 Follow-up

7 ROLE PLAY   *How long have you been . . . ?*

A (PAIR WORK)   Imagine that you are a reporter interviewing your partner for a profile story. Ask questions about past and current interests. Then switch places. Start like this:

A: What things did you like when you were a kid?
B: When I was little, I liked . . .
A: What are you interested in now?
B: Well, lately I've been . . .

B (GROUP WORK)   Take turns telling your group about what your partner has been doing. Try to use some of the phrases in the box below.

began as	has been able to	moved to
first started	has been thinking about	plans to
had	has been working on	wanted to

☰ Language close-up

8 WHAT DID HE SAY?

Watch the video and complete the commentary. Then compare with a partner.

Kai Nagata talks about his career as a reporter.

When I first ......*started*...... off at the CBC, I

.... on the radio side. I went out as a radio

reporter, and I .... all the same news stories

as the TV reporters, but only for audio. Then I ....

.... and moved over to television, and so, for the

last year, I've .... all my stories visually.

In the .... , TV reporters ....

.... rely on a big crew, a big team .... lots of .... ,

complicated equipment. But with .... technology, I ....

.... a whole TV story on my own. I've .... stories for

TV .... just a video camera in my backpack .... a laptop

computer.

9 VERB TENSES *Talking about the past and present*

A Match phrases from A and B and write four sentences. Then compare with a partner.

A	B
Kai has been learning French	since he was a kid.
Kai was promoted to the TV side	since he arrived in Montreal.
Kai has been riding his bike	after working as a radio reporter.
Kai's ancestors immigrated to Canada	when he first joined the CBC.
Kai reported simple stories	more than a hundred years ago.

1. Kai has been learning French since he arrived in Montreal.

2. ....

3. ....

4. ....

5. ....

B Now complete these sentences with information about yourself.
Compare with a partner.

1. I was .... when I ....

2. While I was .... , I became interested in ....

3. I've been .... for the last ....

13 Street performers

Preview

1 CULTURE

Visitors to Boston, Massachusetts should not miss Faneuil (*fan-yule*) Hall Marketplace. It is one of the United States' top tourist sites. This historic marketplace opened in 1742 and was a market and the site of famous meetings. It is near the water, and there are many restaurants and shops for people to enjoy. What makes the marketplace really exciting, though, is the free entertainment. Every day the marketplace fills with street performers and the people who come to watch them.

Faneuil Hall Marketplace

Are street performers popular in your country?
Would you stop to watch a street performer?
Do you think people should give money to street performers? Why or why not?

2 VOCABULARY *Street performers*

A PAIR WORK Write the correct word(s) under each picture.

✓an acrobat	an accordion player	a balloon man	a clown	a dance troupe	a magician

1. ....

2. an acrobat ....

3. ....

4. ....

5. ....

6. ....

B Can you think of four more types of street performers? Write them below.

1. .... 2. .... 3. .... 4. ....

       Interchange VRB 2 © Cambridge University Press 2012 Photocopiable

3 GUESS THE FACTS

Watch the first minute of the video with the sound off. Who is the host?

a reporter   a tour guide   a tourist

Watch the video

4 GET THE PICTURE

Write the type of performer under each picture. Which performers did the host talk to or talk about? Check (✓) the correct answers. Then compare with a partner.

....

....

....

....

5 WATCH FOR DETAILS

What are these people's opinions of the performers? Write at least two words. Then compare with a partner.

....
....
....

....
....
....

....
....
....

WHAT'S YOUR OPINION?

A What do you think of the performers? Rate each performance from 1 (very good) to 5 (poor). Circle the numbers.

1	1	1	1
2	2	2	2
3	3	3	3
4	4	4	4
5	5	5	5

B **PAIR WORK** Compare opinions. Choose words from the box or use words of your own.

amazing	energetic	great	surprised
amusing	entertaining	interesting	talented
boring	excellent	fascinating	unbelievable
creative	fun	silly	

A: What did you think of the balloon man?
B: I thought he was creative. I gave him a 2. How about you? . . .

Follow-up

 HIRE A PERFORMER

GROUP WORK Imagine you are planning a party and want to hire a performer or group of performers. Which of these performers would you like to hire? Why?

A: I think it would be great to hire a magician.
B: Why?
A: Well, because magicians are entertaining. . . .

a mime   **a guitarist**   **a magician**   **a pianist**   **a rock band**

Language close-up

WHAT DID THEY SAY?

Watch the video and complete the interview. Then compare with a partner.

The host asks a woman what she thought of a street performer.

Host: So what did you ....*think*........ about his .... ?

Woman: I .... by what he could do, and all the things he .... make

out of balloons! This man is .... It .... you feel like you're a

.... again. I think .... both really ....

what he's doing. It's .... to .... by someone on the street, and

.... , they're just making something .... out of a ....

PARTICIPLES *Giving opinions*

A Rewrite these sentences using present and past participles. Then compare with a partner.

1. The balloon man entertained me.

   The balloon man was entertaining.
   I was entertained by the balloon man.

2. The musician surprised me.

   ....
   ....

3. The dance troupe energized me.

   ....
   ....

4. The host amused me.

   ....
   ....

B Now change your sentences to give your true opinions. Read them to a partner.

C Complete the chart. Then compare with a partner.

Something you find entertaining	Something you find boring
I find .... entertaining.	....
Something you find amusing	**Something you find surprising**
....	....

Interchange VRB 2 © Cambridge University Press 2012   Photocopiable

Unit 13 ▪ 53

14 The body language of business

Preview

1 CULTURE

Picture yourself riding in an elevator alone. What happens when someone else enters the elevator? Where do you both stand? Do you make eye contact? Where do people stand when there are four people? Imagine that you enter a crowded elevator, face everyone, make eye contact, and smile. What would people do? What would they think about you? There are unspoken rules for riding in an elevator, just as there are cultural rules for how close we stand to people, the gestures we use, and how much eye contact is polite. But there is one gesture that is universally understood: a smile.

In your country, what gesture do you use when you meet someone for the first time? How do you greet an old friend?
What gestures are considered rude?

2 VOCABULARY *Body language*

PAIR WORK Which word do you think best describes the people below? Check (✓) the correct word.

1. ✓ friendly
   ☐ nervous

2. ☐ bored
   ☐ interested

3. ☐ confident
   ☐ lazy

4. ☐ approachable
   ☐ surprised

5. ☐ confused
   ☐ sincere

3 GUESS THE FACTS

Watch the first 30 seconds of the video with the sound off.
What is your first impression of the woman in the job interview?
Write down a few words that describe her body language.

....

Watch the video

4 GET THE PICTURE

Check (✓) the correct answers. Then compare with a partner.

1. The host says you can make a good
   first impression with . . .
   ☐ what you say.
   ☐ your body language.

2. The host says you have seven seconds
   to show . . .
   ☐ your credibility, confidence, and competence.
   ☐ your job skills and professional experience.

5 WATCH FOR DETAILS

Write the correct sentence under each picture. Then compare with a partner.

> ✓Adjust your attitude.   Make eye contact.   Shake hands.   Stand tall.
> Lean in slightly.   Raise your eyebrows.   Smile.

1. ....   2. ....   3. ....   4. ....

5. ....   6. ....   7. Adjust your attitude.

6 WHAT DOES IT MEAN?

What gestures can you use to convey these attitudes? Check (✓) all the correct answers.
Then compare with a partner.

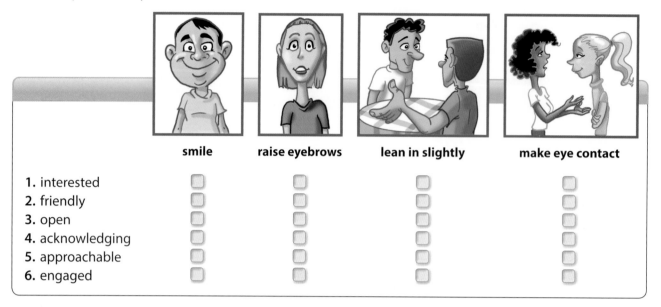

	smile	raise eyebrows	lean in slightly	make eye contact
1. interested	☐	☐	☐	☐
2. friendly	☐	☐	☐	☐
3. open	☐	☐	☐	☐
4. acknowledging	☐	☐	☐	☐
5. approachable	☐	☐	☐	☐
6. engaged	☐	☐	☐	☐

☰ Follow-up

7 GESTURES

A **PAIR WORK** What are some other gestures you might make during
a job interview? Add two gestures to the list. Then compare with a partner.

1. Adjust your attitude.
2. Stand tall.
3. Smile.

4. Make eye contact.
5. Raise your eyebrows.
6. Lean in slightly.

7. Shake hands.
8. ....
9. ....

B Act out each gesture from part A and have your partner
guess which one it is.

8 ROLE PLAY

PAIR WORK Practice making good first impressions.
Take turns acting as the interviewer and interviewee.
Remember to use gestures from the video. Start like this:

A: Hello, I'm (name). (shakes hands)
B: I'm (name). Thank you for coming in. (smiles)

9 WHAT DID SHE SAY?

Watch the video and complete the descriptions. Then compare with a partner.

The host explains some ways to make a positive first impression.

First, adjust your attitude. ....Don't.... ....wait.... until you ....
the interview room to .... Before you ....
through the door, ... about the situation and ....
a conscious choice about the .... you want to embody.
.... that attract .... include .... ,
.... , approachable, and ....

          *   *   *

Make eye contact. .... at someone's .... transmits
energy and indicates .... and ....
.... the interviewer's eyes .... enough to notice
what .... they are. With this one ....
technique, ... dramatically increase ....
likeability factor.

10 MODALS AND ADVERBS *Expressing probability*

A Complete each conversation with a logical answer. Then compare with a partner.

1. A: I just had a job interview. The interviewer didn't offer to shake my hand.
   B: Maybe it means ....

2. A: I sent my friend three text messages, but she didn't respond.
   B: It could mean ....

3. A: My boss was late for our meeting. And she didn't make eye contact at first.
   B: It may mean ....

4. A: I just got this new coat, and I really like it. But sometimes I see people whispering.
   B: Perhaps it means ....

B **PAIR WORK** Now have similar conversations about real or imaginary situations in your own life.

A: My friend Steve doesn't answer my text messages.
B: Maybe it means . . .

Sticky situations

1 CULTURE

In a recent survey, people in the United States were asked to describe their most embarrassing moments during a visit to someone's home. Here are the top answers:

- Dressing incorrectly for the occasion.
- Arriving on the wrong day or wrong time.
- Spilling something or breaking something valuable.
- Saying something by mistake that offended the host.
- Forgetting someone's name.

Almost everyone has dressed the wrong way at least once!

Would the same things be embarrassing in your culture? Why or why not?
What was your most embarrassing moment during a visit to someone's home?

2 VOCABULARY *Problems with guests*

PAIR WORK Do you know these nouns and verbs? Complete the chart. (If you don't know a word, look it up in your dictionary.) Then take turns answering the questions below.

Verb	Noun	Verb	Noun
apologize	apology	misunderstand	
	approval		offer
invite			realization
	lie		reminder

1. Have you apologized for anything recently?
2. What's something a person might lie about?
3. Have you had a problem because someone misunderstood you recently?
4. Has someone offered you something nice recently?
5. Have you had to remind someone to do something lately?

3 GUESS THE FACTS

Watch the video with the sound off. What three embarrassing situations do you see?

Watch the video

4 GET THE PICTURE

A What happened to these people? Write the correct sentence under each picture.

This person didn't like what the host served for dinner.
This person arrived too early for a party.
A dinner guest stayed too late at this person's house.
This person served food her guest didn't like.

A dinner guest stayed too late at this person's house.

Her husband fell asleep at the table.

....

....

....

....

....

....

B Now write one more piece of information under each picture. Compare with a partner.

C PAIR WORK Take turns. Describe what happened to each person.

"This woman invited her boss over for dinner. They had a good time, but her boss wouldn't leave. Her husband fell asleep. . . ."

A What are these people's opinions about the situations? Write the correct number in each box. Then compare with a partner.

Situation 1

The guest should have . . .   The host should have . . .

1. apologized and offered to help.   1. asked the guest to run an errand.
2. pretended to have an errand to run.   2. put the guest to work.
3. left quickly and come back later.

Situation 2

The host should have . . .

1. lied and said she had to get up early.
2. pretended she wasn't tired.
3. reminded her boss it was late.
4. asked her boss to do the dishes.

Situation 3

The guest should have . . .   The host should have . . .

1. gone home before eating.   1. asked her guests if they had food allergies.
2. lied and said she was allergic to seafood. 2. asked her guests to bring food.
3. eaten it anyway.   3. eaten it anyway.

B **PAIR WORK** Which people do you agree with? Take turns sharing your opinions.

A: I agree with her *(points to photo)*. The guest should have . . .
B: I think his suggestion is better *(points)*. The guest should have . . .

☰ Follow-up

6 WHAT WOULD YOU HAVE DONE?

GROUP WORK Take turns describing awkward or embarrassing situations you've been in. Say what you did. Your classmates will tell you what they would have done.

A: I realized I forgot my best friend's birthday, so I gave her some flowers two weeks later and apologized. What would you have done?

B: Well, I think I would have . . .

☰ Language close-up

7 WHAT DID THEY SAY?

People are describing difficult situations involving guests.

A Watch the first situation. Complete the guest's description.

I was .... *invited* .... to a .... , and I .... an hour
.... I thought it would .... me .... to get
there. Well, Rebecca .... to the door .... sweatpants
and an old T-shirt. . . . I could .... the shower .... in the
background, and of course, ... a single guest was ....

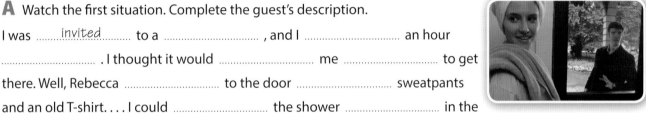

B Now watch the second situation. Complete the host's description.

I .... my boss and her husband to .... the other
.... We had a .... time, but she just wouldn't
.... By .... , my .... and I were so
.... Finally, my husband fell .... at the table. My boss
was very .... when she .... it was so ....
I just .... know what to do when a guest won't go ....

8 WOULD HAVE *AND* SHOULD HAVE *Giving suggestions*

A **PAIR WORK** Can you think of suggestions for these situations? Write statements using **would have** and **should have**. Then compare around the class. Who has the best suggestions?

1. A guest arrived on the wrong day for the party.
   The guest *should have apologized and gone home* .
   If I were the host, I *would have* . . ..

2. A dinner guest broke a valuable dish.
   If I were the guest, I ....
   The host ....

3. Two dinner guests got into a big argument.
   The guests ....
   If I were the host, I ....

4. The host discovered she didn't have enough food.
   The guests ....
   If I were the host, I ....

It's my birthday!

1 CULTURE

In the United States and Canada, birthdays are celebrated at all ages and in different ways. There is no typical party; some are large and others are small. For children, parents throw parties at home or at a child-themed restaurant. Guests are expected to bring presents. For adults, parties are held at home or at a restaurant or club. Presents aren't usually expected, but for parties at home, it's always good to bring some food or drink for the host. Two things you can expect at all birthday parties: a cake with candles and people singing "Happy Birthday to You."

How do people in your country celebrate birthdays?
Are certain birthdays more important to celebrate than others?
What are guests expected to do for a birthday?

2 VOCABULARY *Adjectives*

PAIR WORK How would you feel in the situations below? Choose adjectives from the box.

amused	delighted	enthusiastic	nervous	shy
angry	disappointed	excited	pleased	upset
bored	embarrassed	interested	relaxed	worried

1. You are a dinner guest at someone's house. Your host offers you food you don't like.

   A: I think I'd feel worried. How can I avoid eating it and not offend my host?

   B: Really? I'd be relaxed. Just eat a little bit and say you had a big lunch.

2. Your best friend gives you a gift that you really don't like.

3. Someone forgets an appointment with you.

4. You meet someone you like at a party. The next day you run into the person at the supermarket.

5. Someone talks to you at the store. You realize it's someone you've met before, but you can't remember the person's name.

3 GUESS THE STORY

Watch the first two minutes of the video with the sound off.
What do you think Tim is doing? Check (✓) your answer.

- ☐ trying to make plans
- ☐ trying to get out of plans
- ☐ trying to find someone

☰ Watch the video

4 GET THE PICTURE

How do you think these people really felt? Check (✓) the best answers.
Then compare with a partner.

1. How did Sofia act when she told Tim everyone was busy?
   - ☐ angry
   - ☐ sympathetic

2. How did Tim feel when Steve said he was busy Saturday?
   - ☐ disappointed
   - ☐ pleased

3. Was Sofia pleased with Steve's text message?
   - ☐ definitely
   - ☐ probably not

4. How did Tim feel when he arrived at Sofia's house?
   - ☐ happy to see her, but disappointed that no one else could come
   - ☐ confused that Sofia was the only person there

5. What was Tim's reaction when Sofia turned on the video?
   - ☐ He was angry that his friends surprised him.
   - ☐ He was delighted that his friends surprised him.

Who said what? Check (✓) the person who said each sentence.
Was the person lying, or being sincere? On the line,
write **L** for lying or **S** for sincere. Compare with a partner.

1. Everyone told me they were busy.	☐	✓ .....L....	☐	☐ ....
2. I didn't know you were into salsa dancing.	☐	☐	☐	☐ ....
3. We're on a conference call.	☐	☐	☐	☐ ....
4. John can't come to your dinner Saturday.	☐	☐	☐	☐ ....
5. Maybe you guys can stop by the club afterwards.	☐	☐	☐	☐ ....
6. I guess you'll miss my birthday. Too bad.	☐	☐	☐	☐ ....

☰ Follow-up

6 POLITE RESPONSES

A PAIR WORK Imagine you're talking with friends. Complete the
conversations below with polite responses or excuses. Then act them out.

1. A: Why don't we play chess? It's one of my favorite games!

   B: It's one of my favorite games, too. ....

2. A: Do you want to go see the new science fiction movie on Saturday?

   B: ....

3. A: We're having something special for dinner. I hope you like spicy food!

   B: ....

4. A: What do you think of this poem I wrote?

   B: ....

B Now act out at least two new conversations of your own.
You can make them long or short. Make sure not to hurt your
partner's feelings!

7 WHAT DID THEY SAY?

Watch the video and complete the conversation. Then practice it.

Jessica and John make excuses not to come to Tim's birthday party.

Jessica: John can't come to ....*your*.... ....*dinner*.... Saturday.
I just asked him. And ....
that he has other plans.

John: I did?

Jessica: Yeah, you .... that you were playing
guitar with your .... , uh, someplace. In fact, I was very ....
that you .... playing. Very *surprised*.

John: Oh, yeah. .... , I'm busy . . . playing . . . on Saturday. ....

Tim: .... you weren't in the band anymore.

John: This is my farewell concert. I .... do it.

Tim: I guess you'll miss my birthday. ....

John: Yeah, but I can't .... You know .... it is. Maybe
.... can stop by the club ....

Tim: Sure. Yeah. Thanks. That sounds ....

8 REPORTED SPEECH *He said, she said*

A Report what each person said. Then compare with a partner.

1. "Maybe they can change their plans." (Tim)
   Tim said maybe they could change their plans.

2. "I'm salsa dancing." (Steve)
   ....

3. "I'll make it up to you." (Steve to Tim)
   ....

4. "We're on a conference call." (Jessica)
   ....

5. "John can't come to dinner." (Jessica)
   ....

"I'm salsa dancing."

B CLASS ACTIVITY Ask several classmates what they think of
the things in the box. Write down their answers. Then report
their opinions to the class.

A: What do you think of wrestling?
B: I think it's awful.
A: Tina said she thought wrestling was awful. . . .

| jazz music |
| motorcycles |
| old movies |
| pet costumes |
| vegetarian food |
| wrestling |

This page is intentionally left blank

interchange

FIFTH EDITION

2 B

Workbook

Jack C. Richards

with Jonathan Hull and Susan Proctor

CAMBRIDGE
UNIVERSITY PRESS

This page is intentionally left blank

Contents

Credits

Illustrations

337 Jon (KJA Artists): 4, 22; **417 Neal** (KJA Artists): 1, 16, 67, 84, 90; **Mark Duffin**: 39 (Victrola, telephone), 51; **Thomas Girard** (Good Illustration): 32, 87; **John Goodwin** (Eye Candy Illustration): 36, 94; **Gary Venn** (Lemonade Illustration Agency): 30, 64; **Quino Marin** (The Organisation): 79, 91; **Gavin Reece** (New Division): 85; **Paul Williams** (Sylvie Poggio Artists): 42.

Photos

9 Only time will tell.

1 Complete this passage with the verbs in the box. Use the past, present, or future tense.

☐ buy	☐ drive	☐ do	☐ leave	☐ sell
☐ change	✓ go	☐ have to	☐ sell	☐ use

In many countries nowadays, food shopping takes very little time. In the past, people _____*used to go*_____ to a different shop for each type of item. For example, you _____ meat at a butcher's shop and fish at a fish market. A fruit market _____ fruits and vegetables. For dry goods, like rice or beans, you _____ go to grocery stores. Today, the supermarket or superstore _____ all these things. Once every week or two, people _____ in their cars to these huge stores to buy everything – not only food, but also clothes, electronic goods, furniture, and medicine. But in the future, the way we shop _____ again. Nowadays, people _____ a lot of their shopping online. Soon, maybe, no one _____ home to go shopping. Everyone _____ their computers to order everything online.

2 Choose the correct responses.

1. A: When did people travel by horse and carriage?

   B: _____

   • In the next few years.   • About 100 years ago.   • These days.

2. A: When might doctors find a cure for the flu?

   B: _____

   • Nowadays.   • In the next 50 years.   • A few years ago.

3. A: When did the first man go to the moon?

   B: _____

   • Sometime in the future.   • Today.   • About 50 years ago.

4. A: When is everyone going to buy everything online?

   B: _____

   • In the past.   • Right now.   • Soon.

3 **Complete the sentences. Use the words given and ideas from the pictures.**

1. These days, *people go to the beach for vacation.* (beach)
   In the future, *they might go to space for vacation.* (space)

2. In the past, _____ _____ (collect CDs)
   Nowadays, _____ _____ (listen to music online)

3. A few years ago, _____ _____ (desktop computers)
   Today, _____ _____ (tablets)

4. Fifty years ago, _____ _____ (business suits)
   These days, _____ _____ (casual clothes)

5. Nowadays, _____ _____ (drive their own cars)
   Sometime in the future, _____ _____ (cars that drive themselves)

4 Music is change

A Read the article. How did popular music change?

Music Is Change

Popular music has changed a lot in the last one hundred years in the United States. From jazz to rock to hip-hop, music is always moving forward.

Jazz music began to make its appearance about a century ago in the United States as a fusion of European and African musical forms that people could immediately identify as something very new. Musicians all over the world began to play jazz and to make important contributions from their own musical cultures. An example of this is bossa nova (new beat), which began to emerge in Brazil in the 1950s.

Jazz evolved into Swing in the 1930s and 1940s, with large orchestras playing music that people would dance to. The big bands of Count Basie, Duke Ellington, Benny Goodman, and Artie Shaw were very popular. However, the expense of maintaining large orchestras and changing tastes led to a quite different kind of popular music in the 1950s.

In the 1950s, the rock 'n' roll electric guitar began to replace the jazz horn. Bands with only a guitarist or two, a drummer, and a singer became popular. Of course, the most important singer of this music in the U.S. was Elvis Presley. Like jazz, rock 'n' roll inspired musicians from all over the world, such as the Beatles from England, to make some of the best and most popular songs.

In the 1970s, alternatives to rock 'n' roll began to appear. Three of the most important new sounds were disco, punk, and hip-hop. Disco was famous for the rich sound created by studio musicians and the flashy clothes of the dancers. Punk was a return to small bands that played their own instruments very loud and fast and criticized society in their songs. Hip-hop began as a way to use record players to make music for parties without the need for musicians playing traditional instruments.

Some people say that these musical forms are the "children" of jazz. In any case, they are now played throughout the world with each country contributing its own very particular sound.

B What about you? Answer these questions about your own country's music.

1. What kind of music do you think your grandparents listened to? Do you like this kind of music?

_____

2. Was rock 'n' roll important to your parents? Was there someone like Elvis Presley or the Beatles in your country? Who?

_____

3. What kind of popular music do you listen to? Is it influenced by any of the musical forms discussed in the article? Which ones?

_____

5 Choose the correct responses.

1. **A:** What if I get in shape this summer?

   B: _____

   - You might be able to come rock climbing with me.
   - You won't be able to come rock climbing with me.

2. **A:** What will happen if I stop exercising?

   B: _____

   - Well, you won't gain weight.
   - Well, you might gain weight.

3. **A:** What if I get a better job?

   B: _____

   - You won't be able to buy new clothes.
   - You'll be able to buy some new clothes.

4. **A:** What will happen if I don't get a summer job?

   B: _____

   - You'll probably have enough money for your school expenses.
   - You probably won't have enough money for your school expenses.

6 Verb pairs

A Which words go with which verbs? Complete the chart.

☐ a cold   ☐ money
✓ energetic ☐ relaxed
☐ a group   ☐ time
☐ married   ☐ a gym

feel	get	join	spend
energetic	_____	_____	_____
_____	_____	_____	_____

B Write sentences with *if*. Use some of the words in part A.

1. <u>If I feel energetic, I might go for a walk.</u>
2. _____
3. _____
4. _____
5. _____
6. _____

7 Complete these sentences with your own information. Add a comma where necessary.

> **Grammar note: Conditional sentences with *if* clauses**
>
> The *if* clause can come <u>before</u> or <u>after</u> the main clause.
> **If it comes <u>before</u> the main clause, add a comma.**
> *If I move to a cheaper apartment, I'll be able to buy a car.*
> **If it comes <u>after</u> the main clause, do not add a comma.**
> *I'll be able to buy a car if I move to a cheaper apartment.*

1. If I go shopping on Saturday, <u>I might spend too much money.</u>
2. I'll feel healthier _____
3. If I get more exercise _____
4. If I don't get good grades in school _____
5. I might get more sleep _____
6. I'll be happy _____

8 Nouns and adjectives

A Complete the chart with another form of the word given.

Noun	Adjective	Noun	Adjective
energy	_____	_____	medical
_____	environmental	success	_____
health	_____		

B Complete the sentences. Use the words in part A.

1. There have been a lot of ___medical___ advances in the past half century, but there is still no cure for the common cold.
2. There are a lot of _____ problems in my country. There's too much air pollution, and the rivers are dirty.
3. My _____ is not as good as it used to be. So, I've decided to eat better food and go swimming every day.
4. My party was a great _____. I think I might have another one soon!
5. If I start exercising more often, I might have more _____.

9 **Rewrite these sentences. Find another way to say each sentence using the words given.**

1. Today, people ride bicycles less often than before. (used to)
   People used to ride bicycles more often than they do today. OR
   In the past, people used to ride bicycles more often than they do today.

2. If I stop eating junk food, I may be able to lose weight. (diet)
   _____

3. In the future, not many people will use cash to buy things. (few)
   _____

4. If I get a better job, I can buy an apartment. (be able to)
   _____

5. I'm going to arrive at noon. (will)
   _____

10 **Write three paragraphs about yourself. In the first paragraph, describe something about your past. In the second paragraph, write about your life now. In the third paragraph, write about your future.**

I used to live in a very quiet place . . .

Now, I live in a big city. My job is . . .

If my English improves, I may be able to get a job with an international company . . .

Next year, I'm going to . . . I might . . .

• Paragraph 1 :
My   I used to live in a very quiet place. My house was in a small alley. Neighbors was friendly & very kind. Although, It was near market but It was very quiet. I loved that place. It was all my child hood.

• Paragraph 2 :
I'm living in a city. It's convinient for my job, I can work that I like

_____

_____

_____

_____

_____

_____

10 I like working with people.

1 Choose the correct responses.

1. A: I enjoy working in sales.

B: _____

 • Well, I can. • Neither do I. • So do I.

2. A: I like working the night shift.

B: _____

 • Well, I don't. • Neither do I. • Neither am I.

3. A: I can't stand getting to work late.

B: _____

 • I can't. • Neither can I. • Well, I do.

4. A: I'm interested in using my language skills.

B: _____

 • So am I. • Oh, I don't. • Oh, I don't mind.

2 Complete the sentences with the words and phrases in the box. Use gerunds.

☐ commute   ☐ start her own business   ☑ work under pressure
☐ learn languages ☐ use a laptop   ☐ work with a team

1. Elena enjoys being a journalist. She has to write a news story by 4:00 P.M. every day, but she doesn't mind _working under pressure_____.

2. Takiko is a novelist. He writes all his books by hand because he hates _____.

3. Sarah usually works alone all day, but she enjoys _____, too.

4. Jennifer works for a large company, but she's interested in _____.

5. Pablo has to use Portuguese and Japanese at work, but he's not very good at _____.

6. Annie has to drive to work every day, but she doesn't like _____.

3 **Rewrite these sentences. Find another way to say each sentence using the words given.**

1. I'm happy to answer the phone. (mind)

   I don't mind answering the phone.

2. I can't make decisions quickly. (not good at)

   _____

3. I hate making mistakes. (stand)

   _____

4. I don't enjoy working alone. (with a team)

   _____

4 **Complete these sentences about yourself. Use gerunds.**

On the job or at school

1. I like _meeting people, but I'm a little shy._

2. I can't stand _____

3. I don't mind _____

In my free time

4. I'm interested in _____

5. I'm not interested in _____

At parties or in social situations

6. I'm good at _____

7. I'm not very good at _____

5 **Choose the correct words.**

1. Eric hates waiting in line. He's a very _____ person.
   (impatient / disorganized / punctual)

2. You can trust Marta. If she says she's going to do something, she'll do it.
   She's very _____.
   (hardworking / level-headed / reliable)

3. Kevin isn't good at remembering things. Last week, he missed another
   important business meeting. He's so _____.
   (efficient / forgetful / moody)

6 Job ads on the Internet

A Read these job listings. Match the job titles in the box with the listings below.

_____ flight attendant _____ journalist _____ language teacher _____ stockbroker

JOBSEARCH

find a job

1. Are you hardworking? Do you enjoy using computers? Do you like learning about world news? This job is for you. Must be good at working under pressure. Some evening and weekend work.

2. Must be well organized, energetic, able to make decisions quickly, and good with numbers. Applicants must be level-headed and able to take responsibility for handling other people's money. No weekend work, but some evening work required.

3. No previous experience necessary, but applicant must be willing to work long hours. Successful applicant will also be punctual and reliable. Excellent position for someone who enjoys traveling.

4. Have you studied a foreign language? You may be the right person for this position. Applicants should be comfortable speaking in front of a group and they should be able to communicate well with others.

B What key word(s) in each job ad helped you find the answers in part A?

1. _____
2. _____
3. _____
4. _____

C Which job would be the best for you? The worst? Number them from 1 (the best) to 4 (the worst) and give reasons. List your special experience, preferences, or personal traits.

Job	Reason
_____ language teacher	_____
_____ journalist	_____
_____ flight attendant	_____
_____ stockbroker	_____

I like working with people. **57**

7 Read what these people say about themselves. Then look at the jobs in the box. Choose a job each person should do and a job each person should avoid. Write sentences using *because.*

☐ accountant ☐ detective ☐ lawyer ✓ nurse ☐ salesperson
☐ carpenter ☐ factory worker ☐ marine biologist ☐ model ✓ social worker

> I enjoy helping people, but I can't stand working nights and weekends.

Alan

1. (make a good / could never) _Alan would probably make a good social worker because he enjoys helping people. He could never be a nurse because he can't stand working nights and weekends._

> I really like doing things with my hands. I also enjoy working with wood. I don't enjoy working in the same place every day, and I hate being in noisy places.

Olivia

2. (could / couldn't) _____

> I'm really interested in meeting people, and I enjoy wearing different clothes every day. I'm not so good at organizing my time, and I don't like to argue.

Margo

3. (would make a good / would make a bad) _____

> I'm really good at selling things. I also love helping people. But I'm not so good at solving problems.

Ha-joon

4. (could be / wouldn't make a good) _____

> I love the outdoors and I'm very interested in the sea. I don't like sitting in an office all day, and I'm not good with numbers.

Eddie

5. (would make a good / wouldn't want to be) _____

8 Add *a* or *an* in the correct places.

1. Mike could never be ^a^ nurse or teacher

because he is very short-tempered

and impatient with people. On the

other hand, he's efficient and reliable

person. So he would make good

bookkeeper or accountant.

2. Scott would make terrible lawyer or

executive. He isn't good at making

decisions. On the other hand, he'd

make excellent actor or artist because

he's very creative and funny.

9 Opposites

A Write the opposites. Use the words in the box.

☐ boring	☐ forgetful	☐ late	☐ outgoing
✓ disorganized	☐ impatient	☐ moody	☐ unfriendly

1. efficient / _disorganized_

2. friendly / _____

3. punctual / _____

4. interesting / _____

5. level-headed / _____

6. patient / _____

7. quiet / _____

8. reliable / _____

B Complete the sentences with the words in part A.

1. Mingyu is an _____ person. She really enjoys meeting new people.

2. Hannah is very _____. One day she's happy, and the next day she's sad.

3. I can't stand working with _____ people. I like having reliable co-workers.

4. Charles is an _____ person. I'm never bored when I talk to him.

A Choose the correct word to complete each sentence.

☐ critical	☐ efficient	☐ forgetful	☐ generous
☐ impatient	☐ level-headed	☑ reliable	☐ strict

1. I always do my job well. My boss never has to worry because I'm _____reliable_____.

2. Ed would make a great nurse because he's so _____. He never gets anxious or upset when things go wrong.

3. A good lawyer has to remember facts. Nathan is a terrible lawyer because he's very _____.

4. My favorite teacher at school was Mrs. Wilson. She was pretty _____, so no one misbehaved in her class.

5. My boss is very _____. She gave me a big holiday bonus.

6. June's assistant is very _____. She works fast and never wastes time.

7. My boss complains about everything I do. He's so _____.

8. Julie is so _____. She can't stand waiting for anything.

B Complete the conversations. Use the phrases in the box.

☐ Neither do	☐ Neither am	☐ Neither is	☐ I don't mind
☐ So is	☐ I am	☐ Neither can	☐ So am

1. **A:** I'm not very good at video games. How about you?

   B: Oh, _____. I play video games every weekend.

2. **A:** Jake is not punctual.

   B: _____ Karen. She's always late.

3. **A:** I'm so disorganized!

   B: _____ I. My desk is a mess. I can never find anything.

4. **A:** I don't mind traveling for work.

   B: _____ I. I think it's kind of fun.

5. **A:** I can't stand working in the evening.

   B: _____ I. I prefer to work during the day.

6. **A:** I'm not very outgoing at parties.

   B: _____ I. I'm usually pretty quiet at social events.

7. **A:** I hate taking the train to work.

   B: _____. I usually read or listen to music when I'm on the train.

8. **A:** Stella is really creative.

   B: _____ Robert. He always has great ideas.

11 It's really worth seeing

1 Complete these sentences. Use the passive form of the verbs in the box.

- ☐ compose
- ☐ discover
- ☐ paint
- ☑ design
- ☐ invent
- ☐ write

1. The Niterói Contemporary Art Museum in Brazil _____was designed_____ by the architect Oscar Niemeyer.

2. The play *Romeo and Juliet* _____ by William Shakespeare in the 1590s.

3. The microwave oven _____ by Percy Spencer in 1947.

4. The picture *Sunflowers* _____ by Vincent van Gogh in 1888.

5. In 1960, a 1,000-year-old Viking settlement in Canada _____ by Norwegian explorer Helge Ingstad.

6. The song "Let It Go" from the movie *Frozen* _____ by a married couple, Robert Lopez and Kristen Anderson-Lopez.

2 Change these active sentences into the passive.

1. Scientists first identified the Ebola virus in 1976.

   The Ebola virus was first identified by scientists in 1976.

2. J. J. Abrams directed the box-office hit *Star Wars: The Force Awakens*.

   — The box-office hit Star War: The Force Awakens was directed J.J Abrams

3. The Soviet Union launched the first satellite into space in 1957.

   — The first satellite was launched into space by The Soviet Union in 1957

4. E. B. White wrote the children's novel *Charlotte's Web*.

   — The children's novel Charlotte's web was written by E.B. White

5. Frank Lloyd Wright designed the Guggenheim Museum in New York City.

   — The Guggenheim Museum in New York City was designed by Frank Lloyd Wright

61

3. Write sentences. Use the simple past form of the passive with *by*.

1. Angkor Wat

builder: Suryavarman II
year: 1150

2. the Blue Mosque

designer: Mehmet Aga
year: 1616

3. Buckingham Palace

builder: the Duke of Buckingham
year: 1705

4. Canberra, Australia

planner: Walter Burley Griffin
year: 1913

5. the Vasco da Gama Bridge

designer: Armando Rito
year: 1998

6. the Burj Khalifa

builders: 12,000 workers
year: 2010

The Angkor Wat was builder in 1150 by Suryavarma II (handwritten margin note)

1. Angkor Wat was built by Suryavarman II in 1150.
2. The Blue Mosque was designed by Mehmet Aga in 1616
3. Buckingham Palace was builder by Duke of Buckingham in 1705
4. Canberra, Australia was planned by Walter Burley Griffin in 1913
5. The vasco da Gama Bridge was designed by Armando Rito in 1998.
6. The Burj Khalifa

4 Which city?

A Read about these cities. Write the cities in the box next to the correct descriptions below.

☐ Cusco, Peru   ☐ Bogotá, Columbia   ☐ Valparaíso, Chile
☐ Rio de Janeiro, Brazil   ☐ Montevideo, Uruguay   ☐ Ottawa, Canada

_____ This capital city's name is taken from the word *adawa* in the Algonquin language, which probably means "to trade."

_____ The Spanish explorer Juan de Saavedra named this city after his village in Spain. The name means "Valley of Paradise."

_____ The name of this city, which means "River of January" in English, comes from the fact that it was discovered by the Portuguese on January 1, 1502. However, there's no river in the city, just the bay!

_____ The name of this city comes from the expression *Qusqu Wanka* (Owl of the Rock) in Quechua, the language of the Incas. The myth was that a hero who grew wings discovered the place and then became a rock to mark the spot.

_____ The most popular belief about the name of this city is that it comes from the Portuguese expression *monte vid eu* (I saw a hill), spoken by a sailor who first saw this spot in January of 1520.

_____ The name of this city comes from the indigenous Muisca language, but the original word was *bacatá* (planted fields).

B Check (✓) True or False. For statements that are false, write the correct information.

	True	False
1. Both Bogotá and Ottawa were named after a person.	☐	☐
2. Montevideo and Valparaíso were named by explorers.	☐	☐
3. Cusco was named after the mythological story of a bird.	☐	☐
4. Rio de Janeiro was named because of the month of the year it was discovered.	☐	☐

5 Add *is* or *are* where necessary.

Ecuador ^is^ situated on the equator in the northwest of South America. It made up of a coastal plain in the west and a tropical rain forest in the east. These two areas separated by the Andes mountains in the center of the country.

The economy based on oil and agricultural products. More oil produced in Ecuador than any other South American country except Venezuela. Bananas, coffee, and cocoa grown there. Many of these products exported. Hardwood also produced and exported.

Many people in Ecuador are of Incan origin. Several native languages spoken there, such as Quechua. Spanish spoken in Ecuador, too.

6 Complete the sentences. Use the words in the box.

☑ handicrafts ☐ electronics ☐ peso ☐ wheat
☐ beef ☐ mining ☐ tourism

1. In many countries, _handicrafts_ are sold by people who make them as well as sell them.

2. The _____ is the currency that is used in Chile.

3. Millions of people visit Italy every year. _____ is a very important industry there.

4. A lot of meat, especially _____, is exported by Argentina.

5. Gold _____ is an important industry in South Africa.

6. Much of the world's _____ is grown in the Canadian prairies. It's used to make foods like bread and pasta.

7. A lot of computers are exported by Taiwan. In fact, the _____ industry is an important part of many East Asian economies.

7 Complete this paragraph with *is* or *are* and the past participle of the verbs in the box. Some words may be used more than once.

border	divide	find	locate
call	fill	know	visit

Every year, millions of tourists visit California. California _____ for its beautiful scenery, warm climate, and excellent food. There are many national parks in California. They _____ by over 30 million people every year. Many world-famous museums _____ there, including the Getty Center in Los Angeles and the San Francisco Museum of Modern Art.

The state _____ into two parts, called Northern California and Southern California. San Francisco and Yosemite National Park _____ in Northern California.

San Francisco _____ by water on three sides. It is a city with a beautiful bay and two famous bridges. San Francisco's streets _____ always _____ with tourists. On the north end of the bay is the world-famous Napa Valley. South of San Francisco, there is an area that is famous for its computer industries; it _____ Silicon Valley. Many computer industries _____ there. Los Angeles, Hollywood, and Disneyland _____ in Southern California. Southern California _____ for its desert areas, which are sometimes next to snowcapped mountains.

8 Rewrite these sentences. Find another way to say each sentence using the words given.

1. The designer of the Montjuic Tower in Barcelona was Santiago Calatrava. (designed)

   _____

2. Switzerland has four official languages. (spoken)

   _____

3. In South Korea, a lot of people work in the automobile industry. (employed)

   _____

4. Malaysia has a prime minister. (governed)

9 Wh- questions and indirect questions

A Look at the answers. Write Wh- questions.

1. What _____

The telephone was invented by Alexander Graham Bell.

2. Where _____

Acapulco is located in southern Mexico.

3. When _____

Santiago, Chile, was founded in 1541.

4. What _____

Rice is grown in Thailand.

B Look at the answers. Write indirect questions.

1. Do you know _____

The Golden Gate Bridge is located in San Francisco.

2. Can you tell me _____

Don Quixote was written by Miguel de Cervantes.

3. Do you know _____

Antibiotics were first used in 1941.

4. Could you tell me _____

The tea bag was invented by Thomas Sullivan in 1908.

10 Complete the sentences. Use the passive of the words given.

1804   The first steam locomotive

_____was built_____ (build) in Britain.

1829   A speed record of 58 kph (36 mph)

_____ (establish) by a train

in Britain.

1863   The world's first underground railway

_____ (open) in London.

1964   "Bullet train" service _____

(introduce) in Japan.

1990   A speed of 512 kph (320 mph) _____

(reach) by a French high-speed train.

1995   Maglevs _____ (test) in several countries.

These trains use magnets to lift them above the ground.

2006   The Qinghai-Tibet railway _____ (finish).

It is the world's highest railway and reaches 5,072 meters (16,640 feet).

2011   The journey time from Beijing to Shanghai _____ (reduce)

from 10 hours to 5.5 hours by the new maglev train.

12 It's a long story.

1 Describe what these people were doing when a fire alarm went off in their apartment building last night. Use the past continuous.

Carolyn

Peter

the Mitchells

Isabella and Carlos

Mr. Yang

Paula

1. _Carolyn was washing the dishes when the fire alarm went off._

2. _____

3. _____

4. _____

5. _____

6. _____

2 Describe your activities yesterday. What were you doing at these times?

At 9:00 A.M.

At 9:00 A.M., I was having
breakfast at a coffee shop
with my friends.

About 10:00 last night

_____

_____

_____

In the afternoon

_____

_____

_____

Around noon

_____

_____

_____

At 11:00 in the morning

_____

_____

_____

At this time yesterday

_____

_____

_____

3 Complete the conversation with the correct word or phrase.

Matt: How did you get your first job, Sonia?

Sonia: Well, I _____ got _____ a summer job in a department store
(got / was getting)

while I _____ at the university.
(studied / was studying)

Matt: No, I mean your first full-time job.

Sonia: But that *is* how I got my first full-time job. I _____ during the
(worked / was working)

summer when the manager _____ me a job after graduation.
(offered / was offering)

Matt: Wow! That was lucky. Did you like the job?

Sonia: Well, I did at first, but then things changed. I _____ the same
(did / was doing)

thing every day, and they _____ me any new responsibilities.
(didn't give / weren't giving)

I _____ really bored when another company
(got / was getting)

_____ me to work for them.
(asked / was asking)

4 Look at the pictures and complete these sentences.

1. My roommate was studying when
_she fell asleep!_____

2. I saw an old friend last week while
_____

3. My car was giving me a lot of trouble, so
_____

4. Coffee arrived while
_____

5 One foot in one country, one foot in another

A Scan the article. Why is Lila Downs famous?

Lila Downs

Lila Downs is a Grammy-award winning singer and songwriter who is famous not only in Mexico and the United States, but throughout the world.

Lila was born in the state of Oaxaca, Mexico in 1968. Her mother belongs to the indigenous Mixtec people who speak both Mixtec and Spanish. Her father, who died when Lila was sixteen, was a professor of art and film from the United States. As a girl living in and traveling between Mexico and the U.S., Lila picked up the musical influences that give her music a very international flavor. She still travels a lot between Mexico and the U.S. because her husband is from Minnesota.

Lila is trilingual. She sings in Mixtec, Spanish, and English. She can sing in other languages, too. She learned to sing as a child by listening to her mother, who was a professional singer of Mexican popular music. Lila's first big success came in 1999 with her album *La Sandunga*, which is the name of a traditional dance in Oaxaca. In 2005 she went on to win the Latin Grammy award for *Una Sangre (One Blood)*.

Lila became known to many people through her singing performance in *Frida*, the 2002 film about the famous Mexican artist Frida Kahlo. She has acted in and contributed music to a number of films, while also writing the music and lyrics with her husband to the musical version of *Como agua para chocolate (Like Water for Chocolate)*, based on the very popular book by Mexican novelist Laura Esquivel.

Although she studied classical voice at college in the United States, Lila has devoted a great part of her career to singing the music of Mexico in Spanish, Mixtec, and Zapotec, which is another indigenous language in the state of Mexico. Many of her songs are concerned with social justice.

B Read the article and check (✓) True or False. For statements that are false, write the correct information.

	True	False
1. Lila Downs' father was a professor of literature in the United States.	☐	☐
2. Her husband is from the United States.	☐	☐
3. She wrote the book *Como agua para chocolate*.	☐	☐
4. She studied classical voice in college in Mexico.	☐	☐
5. She speaks Spanish, Mixtec, and English.	☐	☐

6 How long has it been?

A Write sentences. Use the present perfect continuous and *for* or *since*.

> **Grammar note: *for* and *since***
>
> **Use *for* to describe a period of time.**
> *Linda has been living in Seattle **for three months**.*
> *I haven't been jogging **for very long**.*
> **Use *since* to describe a point of time in the past.**
> *Linda has been living in Seattle **since she changed jobs**.*
> *I haven't been jogging **since I hurt my foot**.*

1. Annie / work / actor / three years

   Annie has been working as an actor for three years.

2. Carrie and Alex / go / graduate school / August

   _____

3. Tom / study / Chinese / a year

   _____

4. Linda / not teach / she had a baby

   _____

5. Lori / not live / Los Angeles / very long

   _____

6. Luis and Silvina / travel / South America / six weeks

   _____

B Write sentences about yourself. Use the phrases and clauses in the box (or your own information) and *for* or *since*.

18 months	a few weeks
2006	I was in high school
ages	this morning

1. *I haven't been swimming in ages.*
2. _____
3. _____
4. _____
5. _____
6. _____

7 Look at the answers. Write the questions.

Mark: _What have you been doing lately?_

Andrew: I've been working a lot and trying to stay in shape.

Mark: _____

Andrew: No, I haven't been jogging. I've been playing tennis in the evenings with friends.

Mark: Really? _____

Andrew: No, I've been losing most of the games. But it's fun. How about you?

_____

Mark: No, I haven't been getting any exercise. I've been working long hours every day.

Andrew: _____

Mark: Yes, I've even been working on weekends. I've been working Saturday mornings.

Andrew: Well, why don't we play a game of tennis on Saturday afternoon? It's great exercise!

8 Choose the correct responses.

1. A: When I was a kid, I lived on a farm.

   B: _____

   • Really? Tell me more.

   • Oh, have you?

   • So have I.

2. A: I haven't been ice-skating in ages.

   B: _____

   • Why were you?

   • Wow! I have, too.

   • Neither have I.

3. A: I was a teenager when I got my first job.

   B: _____

   • Really? Where do you work?

   • Really? That's interesting.

   • For five years.

4. A: I haven't seen you for a long time.

   B: _____

   • I didn't know that.

   • Not since we graduated.

   • Hmm, I have no idea.

9 Complete the answers to the questions. Use the past continuous or the present perfect continuous of the verbs given.

1. **A:** Have you been working here for long?

   B: No, I _haven't been working_ (work) here for very long –
   only since January.

2. **A:** Were you living in Europe before you moved here?

   B: No, I _____ (live) in South Korea.

3. **A:** How long have you been studying English?

   B: I _____ (study) it for about a year.

4. **A:** What were you doing before you went back to school?

   B: I _____ (sell) real estate.

5. **A:** What have you been doing since I last saw you?

   B: I _____ (travel) around the country.

10 Rewrite these sentences. Find another way to say each sentence using the words given.

1. Terri was about 15 when she started saving up for a world trip. (teenager)

   Terri started saving up for a world trip
   while she was a teenager.

2. I was getting dressed when my friend arrived. (while)

   _____

   _____

3. I've been a fan of that TV show since I was a kid. (a long time)

   _____

   _____

4. I've had a part-time job for a year. (last year)

   _____

   _____

5. I've been spending too much money lately. (not save enough)

   _____

   _____

6. I haven't seen you for a long time. (ages)

   _____

   _____

13 That's entertainment!

1 **Choose the correct words to complete these movie reviews.**

Classic Movie Review

Login / Register

Home   Reviews   News   Archives   Search

Indiana Jones and the Kingdom of the Crystal Skull

This action movie is dumb. It has

_____amazing_____ (amazed / amazing)

action scenes, but the story is really

_____ (bored / boring). I think

the other Indiana Jones movies were

_____ (excited / exciting), but

I think this one is ridiculous.

Brian's Song

This drama is based on a _____

(fascinated / fascinating) true story. It's about Brian

Piccolo, a football player who develops a terrible

disease, and his friend Gayle Sayers. Maybe

it doesn't sound _____ (interested /

interesting), but it's a must-see. The film has

great acting and a wonderful script. I was very

_____ (moved / moving) by the story of

the friendship between Piccolo and Sayers.

2 **Choose the correct words.**

1. Denzel Washington was __outstanding__ (horrible / ridiculous / outstanding) in his last movie. I think he's a really great actor.

2. I really enjoyed all of the *Hunger Games* movies. In fact, I think they're _____ (terrible / wonderful / boring).

3. The special effects were great in that sci-fi movie we saw last week. They can do such _____ (silly / dumb / incredible) things with 3-D technology these days.

4. The latest *Star Wars* movie was _____ (dumb / disgusting / fantastic), and I'd love to see it again.

3 Choose the correct responses.

1. A: I think that Keira Knightly is very pretty.

  B: *Oh, I do, too.*

   • Oh, I do, too.
   • I don't like her either.

2. A: His new movie is the dumbest movie I've ever seen.

  B: _____

   • Yeah, I liked it, too.
   • I didn't like it either.

3. A: It's weird that they don't show more classic movies on TV. I really like them.

  B: _____

   • I know. It's really wonderful.
   • I know. It's strange.

4. A: I think Tina Fey is hilarious.

  B: _____

   • Yeah, she's horrible.
   • Yeah, she's excellent.

5. A: The movie we saw last night was ridiculous.

  B: _____

   • Yes, I agree. It was exciting.
   • Well, I thought it was pretty good.

4 Write two sentences for each of these categories.

1. Things you think are exciting

 I think paragliding is exciting.

 _____

2. Things you are interested in

 _____

 _____

3. Things you think are boring

 _____

 _____

4. Things you are disgusted by

 _____

 _____

5 Movie classics on the Internet

A Read about these movies available online. Write the number of the movie next to its type.

_____ fantasy   _____ war movie   _____ romantic drama   _____ science fiction

Movie Classics

1. *Casablanca* (1945)
This is the story of two people in love during World War II who are waiting in Casablanca for a chance to escape from the war. Starring Humphrey Bogart and Ingmar Bergman and directed by John Huston, this movie is a must!

2. *Pan's Labyrinth* (2006)
This movie blends a story of the Spanish Civil War with the mythological fantasies of a young girl (Ivana Baquero). It takes place in the mountains of northern Spain where legends of strange creatures are still told. The movie was written and directed by Guillermo de Toro. It is a masterpiece and it is out of this world!

3. *2001: A Space Odyssey* (1968)
Directed by Stanley Kubrick, this is a story about two astronauts who are on a fatal mission in outer space. But it's the ship's computer, HAL, who really steals the show.

4. *The Bridge Over the River Kwai* (1957)
You will never forget the music of this film! And you will understand why many people think it is one of the best movies ever made about war. It is the story of British and American soldiers who are prisoners of war. They must build a bridge in Burma during World War II. You will not be disappointed!

B Write the name of the movie described.

1. a movie with an unusual "star": _____

2. two lovers in a difficult situation: _____

3. where dreams and reality meet: _____

4. its music is unforgettable: _____

C Match the expressions in column A with their meanings in column B.

A	B
1. you won't be disappointed _____	**a.** you need to see it
2. out of this world _____	**b.** becomes the center of attention
3. it's a must _____	**c.** you're going to like it
4. steals the show _____	**d.** outstanding

6 Tell me more!

A Rewrite these sentences. Use *who* or *which*.

1. *The Sound of Music* is a movie. It has been very popular for a long time.

   The Sound of Music is a movie which has been very popular for a long time.

2. *The Theory of Everything* is a movie. It is based on a true story about Stephen Hawking.

   _____

3. Elizabeth Taylor was an actress. She won two Academy Awards.

   _____

4. Akira Kurosawa was a director. He was one of the most influential filmmakers in history.

   _____

5. *The Miracle Worker* is a great movie. It won a lot of awards.

   _____

6. Jennifer Lopez is an actress, a dancer, and a singer. She also appears on TV.

   _____

B Write two sentences like those in part A about movies and entertainers. Use *who* or *which*.

1. _____
2. _____

7 Complete the sentences. Use *that* for things or *who* for people.

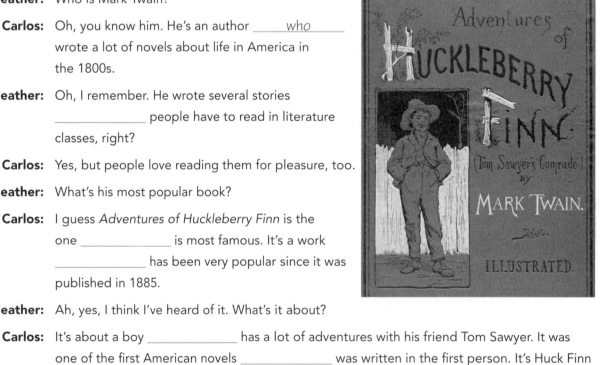

Heather: Who is Mark Twain?

Carlos: Oh, you know him. He's an author _____who_____ wrote a lot of novels about life in America in the 1800s.

Heather: Oh, I remember. He wrote several stories _____ people have to read in literature classes, right?

Carlos: Yes, but people love reading them for pleasure, too.

Heather: What's his most popular book?

Carlos: I guess *Adventures of Huckleberry Finn* is the one _____ is most famous. It's a work _____ has been very popular since it was published in 1885.

Heather: Ah, yes, I think I've heard of it. What's it about?

Carlos: It's about a boy _____ has a lot of adventures with his friend Tom Sawyer. It was one of the first American novels _____ was written in the first person. It's Huck Finn himself _____ tells the story.

Heather: Now, that's a story _____ I'd like to read.

8 Different kinds of movies

A Write definitions for these different kinds of movies. Use relative clauses and the phrases in the box.

☐ has a love story
☑ has cowboys in it
☐ has a lot of excitement
☐ is about a real person
☐ is scary
☐ makes you laugh
☐ shows real events

1. A western *is a movie that has cowboys in it.*

2. A romance _____

3. A comedy _____

4. An action film _____

5. A horror film _____

6. A biography _____

7. A documentary _____

B What kind of movie in part A is your favorite? Your least favorite?
Write one paragraph about each and give reasons for your opinions.

My Favorite Kind of Movie

I really like action movies. They are movies that make me forget about all my problems. . . .

_____

_____

_____

_____

_____

_____

My Least Favorite Kind of Movie

I don't like horror movies because I think they are really dumb. Usually, the story has characters who are not very scary. . . .

_____

_____

_____

_____

_____

_____

_____

9 **Complete these sentences. Use the words in the box.**

☐ character   ☐ composer
☐ cinematography ☐ special effects

1. I thought the _____ in the *Jurassic Park* movies were cool. It's incredible what they can do with computers.

2. Have you ever seen the 1965 film *Doctor Zhivago*? The _____ is beautiful, especially the lighting.

3. Hermione Granger is my favorite _____ in the *Harry Potter* books.

4. I've forgotten the name of the _____ who wrote *Rhapsody in Blue*. Was it George Gershwin?

10 **Rewrite this movie review. Where possible, join sentences with *who, that,* or *which.***

THE HUNGER GAMES

The Hunger Games is a series of science fiction films. They started to come out in 2012. The first one was directed by Gary Ross. He also wrote the screenplay. The films include some famous actors. The actors include Jennifer Lawrence and Woody Harrelson. The films are about a young girl. She is called Katniss. She joins a contest to save her community in the near future. The future is very dark and dangerous. Will she save her community?

The Hunger Games is a series of science fiction films that started to come out in 2012.

_____

_____

_____

_____

_____

Now I get it!

1 What does that mean?

A What do these gestures mean? Match the phrases in the box with the gestures.

a. Stop!
b. I want to turn.
c. We need a taxi.
d. We need help.
e. I'm angry!

1. _e_
2. ___
3. ___
4. ___
5. ___

B Write a sentence about each situation in part A using the phrases in the box.

It could mean . . .   It might mean . . .   It must mean . . .
Maybe it means . . .   Perhaps it means . . .   It probably means . . .

1. _It must mean he's angry._
2. _____
3. _____
4. _____
5. _____

2 Complete the sentences. Use the correct form of the words in the box.

☐ annoy	☐ confuse	☐ embarrass	☐ frustrate
☐ bore	✓ disgust	☐ exhaust	

1. The food in that restaurant is __disgusting__.
   I'll never eat there again!

2. That sign is really _____.
   What does it mean? It's not clear at all.

3. I got stuck behind a really slow bus on a
   narrow mountain road. I felt
   _____ because I couldn't
   pass it.

4. I drove for eight hours on a straight, flat road
   where the scenery never changed. I've never
   been so _____!

5. I couldn't get into the parking space,
   and everyone was looking at me. It was
   pretty _____.

6. I went bicycling all day. Now I'm so
   _____ that I'm going to sleep
   for 12 hours!

7. I asked the taxi driver to turn off his radio
   because the loud music was very
   _____.

3 What would you say in each situation? Use the sentences in the box.

☐ Come here.	☐ Shh. Be quiet!
☐ That sounds crazy!	☐ Where's the restroom?

1. Your friend wants to dye his hair green and wear orange contact lenses.
   _____

2. You can't concentrate on the movie because the people in front of you are talking.
   _____

3. You wave to your friend because you want to show her something interesting.
   _____

4. You just ordered a meal and want to wash your hands before you eat.
   _____

4 Proverbs

A Match the proverbs with their meanings.

Proverbs

1. The grass is always greener on the other side of the fence.

2. An ounce of prevention is worth a pound of cure.

3. An apple a day keeps the doctor away.

4. There are plenty of fish in the sea.

5. Better late than never.

6. Birds of a feather flock together.

Meanings

_____ If you eat the right food you will be healthy.

_____ People with the same interests become friends.

__1__ We may think we will be happier in a different situation, but it is not necessarily true.

_____ Don't worry if you love someone who doesn't return your love. You can always find someone else.

_____ It is easier to fix something before there is a problem than after the problem has occurred.

_____ It is preferable to do something with some delay than to never do it at all.

B What would you say? Choose a proverb for each situation.

1. A: I really don't understand what Miriam sees in Bill.

   B: Oh, I do. They both love movies from other countries and they like learning languages.

   A: Ah, I see! _____

2. A: It's 10 o'clock already! Do you think I can get to the party on time?

   B: That depends on whether you can catch the bus.

   A: But what if I don't?

   B: Well, getting there is the important thing. _____

3. A: A penny for your thoughts.

   B: I was just thinking about what it's like to be a movie star.

   A: Do you think they're any happier than you are?

   B: They must be, don't you think?

   A: Oh, I don't know. _____

4. A: It's cold outside. Why don't you put on your new coat?

   B: Do you think I need to, dear?

   A: Well, you don't want to catch a cold like the one you had last month, do you?

   B: OK, you're right. Like they say, _____

5 What do you think these proverbs mean?

1. Don't cry over spilled milk.

   It could mean _____

2. Don't judge a book by its cover.

   Maybe it means _____

3. There's no such thing as a free lunch.

   It might mean _____

4. Bad news travels fast.

   It probably means _____

6 Complete the conversation. Use each phrase in the box only once.

☐ it might be
☐ it's definitely
☐ you can
☐ you have to
☑ you're not allowed to

Teacher: OK, class. This afternoon, we're going to take the school bus to the science museum.

Student 1: Great! I'm going to take some photos.

Teacher: I'm afraid _you're not allowed to_ take photos.

Student 1: But how can they stop me? I'll use my cell phone, not a camera.

Teacher: _____ check all your things with security.

Student 2: Can I take my jacket into the museum?

Teacher: I'm not sure. _____ best to leave it on the bus.

Student 2: But what about my wallet? It might not be safe on the bus.

Teacher: Oh, _____ a good idea to keep your money with you.
Keep it in your pocket.

Student 3: And what about touching things in the museum?

Teacher: There are "Don't touch!" signs next to some of the things.
But _____ touch things if there is no sign.

7 Look at the numbered photos of signs below. Then complete
the conversations between a driving instructor and his student.
Use each word or phrase in the box only once.

☐ are allowed to	☐ can	☐ don't have to
☑ aren't allowed to	☐ can't	☐ have to

1. **Student:** This is great!

   Instructor: Hey, slow down! You _aren't allowed to_
   go above the speed limit.

2. **Student:** Uh, what does that sign mean?

   Instructor: It means you _____
   turn left.

3. **Instructor:** You look confused.

   Student: What . . . what does that sign mean?

   Instructor: It means you _____
   do two things. You _____
   turn right or go straight.

4. **Instructor:** Why are you stopping?

   Student: The sign says to stop.

   Instructor: Actually, you _____
   stop. Just be prepared to, if necessary.

5. **Instructor:** Hey, stop! Didn't you see that sign?
   It means you _____
   come to a complete stop.

   Student: What sign? I didn't see any sign.

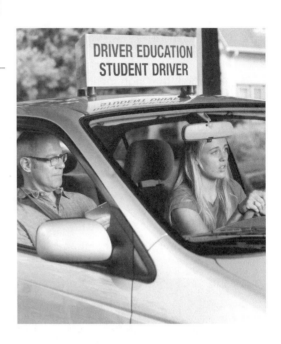

8 Rewrite these sentences. Find another way to say each sentence using the words given.

1. Maybe it means you're not allowed to fish here. (may)

   It may mean you're not allowed to fish here.

2. You can't light a fire here. (allowed)

   _____

3. Perhaps that sign means you're not allowed to swim here. (might)

   _____

4. I think that sign means you can get food here. (probably)

   _____

5. You need to be quiet after 10:00 P.M. (have got to)

   _____

9 Complete each conversation using the words in the box.

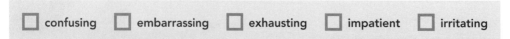
☐ confusing   ☐ embarrassing   ☐ exhausting   ☐ impatient   ☐ irritating

1. **A:** I went to the movies last night. A couple who sat behind me talked during the entire movie.

   B: That's _____!

2. **A:** I fell asleep during class this afternoon. The teacher had to wake me up.

   B: Oh, that's _____!

3. **A:** I drove all night to get there on time.

   B: Oh, that's _____! How can you keep your eyes open?

4. **A:** Did Sara give you directions to the party?

   B: She did, but they're really _____. Hey, can I get a ride with you?

5. **A:** This movie is taking forever to download. Why does it have to take so long?

   B: You are so _____! There, look. It's done!

15 I wouldn't have done that.

1 I think I'd . . .

A What would you do in these situations? Check (✓) an answer or write your own suggestion.

1. Your classmate leaves her new smartphone in the classroom.
   - ☐ run after her and give it back to her immediately
   - ☐ take it home overnight to try it out
   - ☐ _____

2. Someone climbs through your neighbor's window.
   - ☐ call the police
   - ☐ ring the doorbell
   - ☐ _____

3. Your boss makes things difficult for you at work.
   - ☐ talk to your boss
   - ☐ look for another job
   - ☐ _____

4. A friend sounds unhappy on the phone.
   - ☐ ask your friend if he or she has a problem
   - ☐ tell jokes to make your friend laugh
   - ☐ _____

B Write about what you would do in the situations in part A. Use the phrases in the box.

I'd . . .	I might . . .	I guess I'd . . .
I'd probably . . .	I think I'd . . .	

1. If my classmate left her new smartphone in the classroom, I think I'd run after her and give it back to her immediately.

2. _____

3. _____

4. _____

2 Complete these sentences with information about yourself.

1. If a relative asked to borrow some money, I'd _____

2. If I had three wishes, _____

3. If I could have any job I wanted, _____

4. If I had a year of vacation time, _____

5. If I could change one thing about myself, _____

3 Choose the correct word.

1. I'd go ___straight___ to the police if I saw someone breaking into a house.
   (seriously / simply / straight)

2. My friend _____ to cheating on the biology exam, but his teacher still failed him.
   (returned / confessed / said)

3. I'm in a difficult _____ at work. I don't know whether to talk to my boss about it or just quit.
   (divorce / predicament / problem)

4. If I saw someone _____ in a store, I'd tell the store manager immediately.
   (cheating / shoplifting / shopping)

5. My uncle died and left me $20,000. I'm going to _____ most of it.
   (invest / return / sell)

6. When I went back to the parking lot, I tried to get into someone else's car _____ mistake.
   (by / in / with)

7. There is so much great music to download from the Internet. I don't know what to _____.
   (choose / confess / fix)

8. My aunt won't let me use her car because she thinks I'm a terrible driver.
   She has a _____. I had two accidents last year!
   (flat tire / point / reward)

4 What to do?

A Read the article. Match what happened to a possible action.

What happened

1. You bought a camera on sale at a store, but it didn't work right. The salesclerk said, "We can't do anything about it."

2. You checked your bank statement and noticed that there was a deposit of $1,000. You didn't make the deposit. You're sure it was a bank error.

3. You sat on a park bench that had wet paint on it. You ruined your clothes. There was no "Wet Paint" sign.

4. You were not happy with the grade you got in an important class.

5. Your next-door neighbors borrowed your vacuum cleaner. When they returned it, it was damaged.

6. A friend gave you an expensive vase for your birthday, but you didn't really like it.

Possible actions

_____ I guess I'd take it back to the store and exchange it for something else.

_____ I guess I'd write a letter of complaint to the manufacturer.

_____ Maybe I'd ask them to repair it.

_____ I think I'd make an appointment to see the instructor to talk about it.

_____ I'd probably wait until the next month to see if the mistake is corrected.

_____ I'd write a letter to the city council and ask them to pay for the damage.

B What would you do in each situation? Write another possible action.

1. _____

2. _____

3. _____

4. _____

5. _____

6. _____

5 What would you have done in these situations?
Use *would have* or *wouldn't have*.

1. Lisa had dinner in a restaurant and then realized she didn't have any money. She offered to wash the dishes.

   I wouldn't have washed the dishes. I would have
   called a friend to bring me some money.

2. Alex was on a bus when the woman next to him started talking loudly on a cell phone. He asked her to speak more quietly.

   _____

   _____

3. Ryan invited two friends to dinner on Friday, but they came on Thursday by mistake. He told them to come back the next day.

   _____

   _____

4. Luke's neighbors had their TV on very loud late at night. Luke called and complained to the police.

   _____

   _____

5. Sharon had a houseguest who was supposed to stay for three days, but the woman was still there three weeks later. Sharon finally gave her a bill for her room and board.

   _____

   _____

6. Margo accidentally broke a glass at a friend's house. She decided not to say anything about it.

   _____

   _____

6 Write two things you should have done or shouldn't have done
last week, last month, and last year.

1. Last week: _Last week, I should have . . ._ _____

   _____

2. Last month: _____

   _____

3. Last year: _____

   _____

7 Advice column

A Complete each letter with the correct forms of the verbs in each box.

☐ borrow	☐ disagree	☑ marry	☐ spend
☐ deny	☐ enjoy	☐ save	☐ lose

✉ **Ask Harriet**

Dear Harriet,

I've never written to an advice columnist before, but I have a big problem. I'm going out with this really nice guy. He's very sweet to me, and I really want to _____marry_____ him. In fact, we plan to have our wedding next summer. But he has a problem with money. He _____ money like crazy! Sometimes he _____ money from me, but he never pays it back. I want to _____ money because I want us to buy an apartment when we get married. However, if I tell him he has a problem with money, he _____ it. He says, "I _____ with you. You never want to go out and _____ yourself." I don't want to _____ him, but what can I do? – J. M., Seattle

☐ accept	☐ admit	☑ agree
☐ find	☐ forget	☐ refuse

Dear J. M.,

You and your boyfriend must _____agree_____ on how you spend your money *before* you get married. If you both _____ that there is a problem, you could probably _____ an answer. He should _____ your idea of saving some money. And you shouldn't always _____ to go out and have fun. Don't _____ that talking can really help.

Good luck! – Harriet

B What advice would you give J. M.? Write a reply to her letter.

_____

_____

_____

_____

_____

8 To accept or to refuse?

A Complete the conversation with *would* or *should* and the correct tense of the verbs given.

Carly: Guess what, Kristin! A university in New Zealand has offered me a scholarship.

Kristin: Great! When are you going?

Carly: That's just it. I may not go. What _____would_____ you _____do_____ (do) if your boyfriend asked you not to go?

Kristin: Well, I _____ (try) to convince him that it's a good opportunity for me.

Carly: I've tried that. He said I could study the same thing here.

Kristin: If I were you, I _____ (talk) to him again. You know, I once missed a big opportunity.

Carly: Oh? What happened?

Kristin: I was offered a job in Los Angeles, but my husband disliked the idea of moving, so we didn't go. I _____ (take) the job. I've always regretted my decision. In my situation, what _____ you _____ (do)?

Carly: Oh, I _____ (accept) the offer.

Kristin: Well, there's the answer to your predicament. Accept the scholarship!

B What would you do if you were Carly? Why?

If I were Carly, . . . _____

_____

9 What would you do if you found a diamond ring? Complete these sentences.

1. I would _hide it and come back for it later._____
2. I wouldn't _____
3. I could _____
4. I might _____
5. I might not _____

16 Making excuses

1 **People are making many requests of Eric. Write the requests.
Use *ask*, *tell*, or *say* and reported speech.**

1.	**Mark:**	"Eric, take my phone calls."
2.	**Julie:**	"Can you do an Internet search for me, Eric?"
3.	**Andrew:**	"Could you check this flash drive for viruses?"
4.	**Tanya:**	"Eric, put this information on a spreadsheet."
5.	**Carla:**	"Don't forget to add paper to the copier, Eric."
6.	**Alan:**	"Reformat this text file as a PDF file."
7.	**Bruce:**	"Get me some coffee, Eric."
8.	**Cindy:**	"Make five copies of the agenda before the meeting."
9.	**Jack:**	"Could you give me a ride home?"
10.	**Robin:**	"Don't be late to work again."

1. Mark told Eric to take his phone calls.

2. _____

3. _____

4. _____

5. _____

6. _____

7. _____

8. _____

9. _____

10. _____

2 Nouns and verbs

A Complete the chart.

Noun	Verb		Noun	Verb
acceptance	accept		_____	explain
_____	apologize		_____	invite
_____	complain		_____	offer
_____	excuse		_____	suggest

B Complete these sentences. Use the correct form of the words from part A.

1. This coffee tastes awful. I'm going to ___complain___ to the waiter about it.

2. I _____ an invitation to Billy and Kate's house for dinner.

3. I didn't want to go to Jenny's party, so I made up an _____.

4. I was rude to my teacher. I must _____ to him.

5. Can you _____ the end of the movie? I didn't understand it.

6. Steve said he'd take me to the airport. It was really nice of him to _____.

7. Thank you for your helpful _____ on how to fix my essay. The teacher really liked it!

8. I received an _____ to Mindy's party. I can't wait to go.

3 Choose the correct verb. Use the past tense.

☐ express   ☐ give   ☐ make   ☑ offer   ☐ tell

1. Jennifer told me she was graduating from college, so I ___offered___ her my congratulations.

2. I _____ a complaint to the police because our neighbors' party was too noisy.

3. I couldn't go to the meeting, so I _____ my concerns in an email.

4. Jake _____ an excuse for being late for work. He said there had been a traffic jam on the highway.

5. Lori was very funny at the class party. As usual, she _____ a lot of jokes.

What a great excuse!

A Read the invitations and excuses in these text messages between Eileen and William. Underline the phrases that are invitations or excuses.

Hi, William. It would be wonderful if you could come to our party next Friday! It's Mick's birthday and I really think that he would appreciate it if you could be there. All of his friends will be there. The best part is that Mick doesn't know everyone is going to be there. It's a surprise birthday party! So please come and be part of the surprise.

Hi, Eileen. Thank you for the invitation. You know I would love to come if I could, but unfortunately I am working late on Friday. I have to study for my examination next week. So, have a great time without me, and of course I will send a present to Mick.

Oh, William, come on! Please come. The best present you can give to Mick is being with him on his birthday. I know everyone would really enjoy seeing you, too.

Eileen, I really should study for the test. I know I will probably regret not going, but I think I should stick to my plan.

William, you are so right when you say you will regret it if you don't come to Mick's birthday party. All of your friends will be there. As a matter of fact, I mentioned you to Penelope and she said she is looking forward to talking to you at the party. We will all be disappointed if you don't come. Especially Penelope!

Eileen, I've given it some thought and you are right! I should go to Mick's party. In fact, wild horses couldn't stop me. See you on Friday!

B Read the phrases that you underlined. Answer these questions.

1. Why did Eileen text William?
2. Why can't William come to the party?
3. Why do you think William decided to accept the invitation after all?

5 Sorry, but . . .

A The teacher wants to have a class picnic on Saturday. Look at the excuses that students gave her. Change each excuse into reported speech using *say*.

1. Tim: "I'm getting my hair cut."

   Tim said he was getting his hair cut.

2. Teresa: "My sister is having a baby shower."

   _____

3. Bill: "I may have some houseguests on Saturday."

   _____

4. Miyako and Yoshiko: "We're going camping this weekend."

   _____

5. Marco: "I'm sorry, but I'll be busy on Saturday afternoon."

   _____

B Change these excuses into reported speech using *tell*.

1. Abbie: "I signed up for a scuba diving class."

   Abbie told her she had signed up for a scuba diving class.

2. Paul and James: "We'll be moving to our new apartment that day."

   _____

3. Luis: "I watch the football game on TV every Saturday."

   _____

4. Sandra: "I've already made plans to do something else."

   _____

C Write excuses for three more students. Use your own ideas.

1. _____

2. _____

3. _____

6 What did they say?

A Match the reports of what people said in column A with the descriptions in column B.

A	B
1. Sam said that he was talking to Jim in the office for an hour. He's very unhappy about the new company rules. _c_	**a.** giving a reason
2. Brian said that the game was canceled because of bad weather. _____	**b.** refusing an invitation
3. Nina said she would be studying on Saturday night. (But she'll actually be at the movies.) _____	**c.** making a complaint
4. Carl told me he couldn't come for dinner on Friday. He said he had to work late. _____	**d.** telling a lie
5. Max told me that he didn't want to go to the party because Kayla would be there. _____	**e.** making an excuse

B Write each person's original words.

1. Sam: _"I was talking to Jim in the office for an hour. He's very unhappy_
about the new company rules."

2. Brian: _____

_____

3. Nina: _____

_____

4. Carl: _____

_____

5. Max: _____

_____

7 Choose the correct responses.

1. **A:** We're going to go hiking. Do you want to join us?

   B: _____
   - Sorry, I won't be able to.   • What's up?

2. **A:** I'm really sorry. We'll be out of town this weekend.

   B: _____
   - I've made other plans.   • No problem.

3. **A:** Meet us at 7:00. OK?

   B: _____
   - Oh, that's all right.   • OK, sounds like fun.

4. **A:** I'm sorry. I won't be able to make it.

   B: _____
   - Well, never mind.   • Great.

8 Yes or no?

A Which expressions would you use to accept an invitation? To refuse an invitation? Check (✓) the correct answer.

	Accept	Refuse
1. I'm really sorry.	☐	☐
2. Great.	☐	☐
3. Sounds like fun.	☐	☐
4. I've made other plans.	☐	☐
5. I won't be able to make it.	☐	☐
6. I'm busy.	☐	☐
7. Thanks a lot.	☐	☐
8. I'd love to.	☐	☐

B Use the expressions in part A to accept or refuse these invitations. Offer an excuse if you refuse.

1. Would you like to come to a soccer match with me tomorrow?

   _____

2. That new action movie looks great! Do you want to see it with me?

   _____

3. A friend asked me to go to the mall after class. Do you want to join us?

   _____